PENGUIN
COMPASS

DOJO WISDOM FOR WRITERS

Jennifer Lawler is a writer and martial arts expert. She has taught writing and literature at the University of Kansas and she is the former co-chair of the Book Division of the National Writers Union. A frequent speaker at writers' conferences and writing workshops across the country, she is the author of more than twenty books, including *Dojo Wisdom,* which won the American Society of Journalists and Authors Outstanding Book Award in 2004, and her articles have appeared in *Family Circle, American Fitness, New Living* and other magazines. She is a second-degree black belt in Tae Kwon Do and she has taught the martial arts and self-defense for many years. She lives in Lawrence, Kansas, with her daughter.

Dojo Wisdom for Writers

100 Simple Ways
to Become a More Inspired,
Successful and Fearless Writer

Jennifer Lawler

PENGUIN COMPASS

PENGUIN COMPASS
Published by the Penguin Group
Penguin Group (USA) Inc., 375 Hudson Street, New York, New York 10014, U.S.A.
Penguin Books Ltd, 80 Strand, London WC2R 0RL, England
Penguin Books Australia Ltd, 250 Camberwell Road, Camberwell, Victoria 3124, Australia
Penguin Books Canada Ltd, 10 Alcorn Avenue, Toronto, Ontario, Canada M4V 3B2
Penguin Books India (P) Ltd, 11 Community Centre,
Panchsheel Park, New Delhi – 110 017, India
Penguin Books (NZ) Ltd, Cnr Airborne and Rosedale Roads,
Albany, Auckland 1310, New Zealand
Penguin Books (South Africa) (Pty) Ltd, 24 Sturdee Avenue,
Rosebank, Johannesburg 2196, South Africa

Penguin Books Ltd, Registered Offices:
80 Strand, London WC2R 0RL, England

First published in Penguin Compass 2004

1   3   5   7   9   10   8   6   4   2

LIBRARY OF CONGRESS CATALOGING-IN-PUBLICATION DATA
Lawler, Jennifer, 1965–
Dojo wisdom for writers : 100 simple ways to become a more inspired,
successful and fearless writer/ Jennifer Lawler.
p.   cm.
ISBN 0-14-219631-2
1. Authorship—Vocational guidance.   2. Authorship.   I. Title.
PN151.L39 2004
808'.02'023—dc22   2004040090

Printed in the United States of America
Set in Guardi

For Bridget, who believed

Acknowledgments

This book would not have been possible without the support of my many friends in the National Writers Union, including but not limited to that rambunctious lot on the book authors' listserv. I wish you tremendous writing success and *huge* advances.

My agent, Carol Susan Roth, was instrumental in helping me shape this book, and deserves my undying gratitude for finding me when I most needed to be found. My editors at Penguin Putnam, Lucia Watson and Janet Goldstein, are a dream—every writer should be so lucky. They deserve my special thanks. Of course, I have to thank Ann Mah for acquiring me (or at least my books) in the first place. Without her, I would still be writing books with titles like *Dim Mak Death Touch in Twelve Easy Steps*. And Maria Wong deserves special recognition for being a terrific publicist who fortunately understands the true nature of my genius.

Several writers contributed to the cause, practically writing the book for me. The beer's on me next time we meet. Some of you went way, way beyond the call of duty (you know who you are) and deserve an entire *keg* of beer, although not all at once:

Bev Bachel, a writer and business consultant, is an expert on goal-setting, especially for writers, and the founder of Idea Girls. Her website is www.ideagirls.com.

Debz Buller teaches yoga, martial arts and meditation classes in the Kansas City area. She writes books and articles on these subjects and others, such as self-sufficient living, energy healing and the spiritual quest, and volunteers healing work with Veronica's Voice, a group dedicated to assisting prostituted and exploited women into recovery. For more information, check www.samadhigrl.com or email her at samadhigrl@yahoo.com.

Samantha Clark is a writer and artist living in Albuquerque, New Mexico.

Linda Formichelli has written for more than one hundred magazines and is co-author of *The Renegade Writer: A Totally Unconventional Guide to Freelance Writing Success* (Marion Street Press, 2003). Linda also studies Okinawa Hon Karate-do. You can contact her at www.twowriters.net or www.renegadewriter.com.

Maggie Frisch edits and publishes *Working Writer*, a publication offering solid information with a good dose of humor and writing camaraderie. For a free copy of the latest issue, send a request to workingwriters@aol.com, or check out www.workingwriter1.com.

Ruth Gruen, a writer and PR expert, formerly co-owned a publishing company.

Randy Peyser, the author of *Crappy to Happy: Small Steps to Big Happiness NOW!* (RedWheel/Weiser, 2002), helps authors find publishers, edits books and proposals, and offers freelance writing services. For more: www.randypeyser.com.

Jennie Schacht is founder and principal of Schacht and Associates (www.schachtandassociates.com), a consultancy serving the food and health care industries. Ms.

Schacht provides program development, funder research and evaluation to public, for-profit and non-profit organizations and her articles appear in local, national and international publications and on the Web.

Mary Shafer, a full-time freelance writer, makes her living writing commerical copy, articles for trade and consumer magazines, and books under the aegis of her company, The Word Forge. Learn more about Mary at www.thewordforge.com.

Bob Spear is a professional book reviewer and editor and the author of nine nonfiction books on self-defense and personal security (www.heartlandreviews.com and www.sharpspear.com). A 7th degree black belt in the Korean art of Hapkido, he has trained over 11,000 people throughout the world in self-defense. He also writes fiction and owns the Book Barn in Leavenworth, Kansas. He may be contacted at heartlandreviews@kc.rr.com.

Miryam Ehrlich Williamson specializes in translating from medical jargon into plain English. Her most recent books are *Blood Sugar Blues: Overcoming the Hidden Dangers of Insulin Resistance* (Walker, 2001) and *Type 2: A Book of Support* (Walker, 2003), sold online and in bookstores. Find out more: www.mwilliamson.com.

Thanks also to my coffee-and-commiseration team: Julie Mettenburg and Mary O'Connell, two fine writers who have helped me see the value of what I do. Thanks also to Tom Lorenz, writing prof and cheerleader, for encouragement during tentative times.

As always, I must thank my martial arts teachers and colleagues. Masters Donald and Susan Booth started me on the way; Grandmaster Woo Jin Jung keeps me on the straight and narrow; and Dr. Richard Hackworth remains a loyal and dedicated supporter.

And of course I have to thank my daughter, Jessica, for putting up with Mama "lurking" all day long. Now I can finally play, little one.

Contents

Acknowledgments   vii

Introduction   xvii

 1. Find a teacher   1

 2. Trust your teacher   3

 3. Respect the centerline   6

 4. From your Chi flows your creativity   8

 5. Meditate   10

 6. Be open to what happens next   12

 7. Respect your opponent   15

 8. Keep the beginner's mind   18

 9. No knowledge is useless   19

10. Perseverance brings rewards   22

11. Flexibility is strength   23

12. A warrior masters many techniques   26

13. Discipline leads to strength   28

14. Know your target   30

15. Teach others and you will learn   32

16. Physical strength creates mental and
    emotional strength   34

17. The relaxed fist is stronger than the tense one   36

18. Understand what is expected of you   40

19. Courtesy reveals your strength   42

20. Integrity in all actions creates confidence   45

21. The warrior does not reflect on past deeds while in battle   47

22. Know the vital points   49

23. A strike is stronger than a push   51

24. Mastery requires patience   52

25. Cultivate perfect awareness   54

26. Do not fear the blow   56

27. Your beliefs guide your strategy   58

28. Self-consciousness prevents action   60

29. *Aiki,* the impassive mind, brings strength 63

30. Persist even when you are fatigued   65

31. One who is humble can never be overcome   67

32. Push beyond your limits   69

33. Master the present   71

34. Understand the nature of yin-yang   73

35. Take small risks to build courage for large risks   75

36. You cannot fail if you keep trying   77

37. Act on your intention   79

38. Focus on the Way   81

39. Chi overcomes obstacles   84

40. Face the tiger   86

41. Overcome fear by encountering it   88

42. The Way is not always straight   90

43. Catch sight of your reflection   92

44. Seek to be connected with the universe   95

45. Know when to yield and when to stand your ground   96

46. A warrior must be single-minded   98

47. Keep your power quiet   100

48. Disharmony destroys focus   103

49. Let your intuition speak   105

50. Don't give away your moves   107

51. The Way shows itself differently for everyone   109

52. Protect the beginner   111

53. Do what is right   113

54. Choose the path; never look back   114

55. Someone else's win is not always your loss   116

56. Accept criticism to grow   118

57. You can do more than you believe possible   120

58. Hone unexpected skills   121

59. Focus on the openings   123

60. Draw out the guard   125

61. Do not be surprised when the scorpion stings   127

62. Practice daily, regardless of circumstances   129

63. Commit to training   130

64. Strive for mastery   132

65. No one gets the jump spinning wheel kick on the first try   133

66. Find your passion   135

67. Heart is more important than talent   137

68. Observe without judging   139

69. Know yourself   141

70. Accept hard challenges   143

71. Obstacles are opportunities   144

72. Give your strongest effort with every try   147

73. Never let fear create inaction   148

74. Nurture yourself   150

75. See the target beyond the target   151

76. Trust yourself   154

77. Act instead of hoping   156

78. Limit unhealthy choices   157

79. You need a training partner   160

80. Learn from watching   162

81. Understand what you observe   163

82. Sometimes, remain silent   165

83. Find your rhythm 167

84. Practice broken rhythm training 169

85. Explore other styles 171

86. Take what you can use, discard the rest 173

87. Finish the fight 175

88. Smile when you spar 177

89. Use the right equipment 179

90. Imagination is a weapon 181

91. When you enter the *dojo*, abandon your worries 183

92. Your power improves every day 185

93. Your voice is powerful 187

94. Accept differences 188

95. Never reveal your strategy 190

96. Don't allow your opponent to control the match 192

97. Practice your kicks 10,000 times 193

98. The Master respects his profession 195

99. Adventure feeds the spirit 196

100. Create 197

Conclusion 199

Resources 201

Introduction

Like thousands of other people—make that *millions* of other people—I always dreamed of becoming a writer. I love putting words on paper and arranging them just so, and sharing my thoughts and ideas with readers in ways that might make them laugh or cry or at least scratch their heads and think.

But like many aspiring writers, I had a tough time making my dream a reality. I wasn't exactly anyone's precocious protégé. In fact, I'm what you call a late bloomer because it took me so long to figure it all out. I wish I'd known what it takes to be successful a little sooner.

I was five years old when I decided I wanted to make my living writing books. It's the only thing that has never changed about me. As I grew older, friends and family let me know how difficult it was to make a living as a writer. Becoming a writer, it seemed, was not a very practical plan. I listened to everyone else who told me what I should do instead, and I tried that for a while.

But what I really wanted was to be a writer.

As a teenager and young adult, I attempted to make my dream come true, but something always held me back from success. I would write a novel or an essay and then put it in a drawer. I would send a few query letters out and then stop. I'd go do something else. It was amazing the things I thought up to do that interfered with my becoming a writer. I unloaded trucks, I sold insurance, I went to graduate school—all the while promising myself that some-day I would become a writer. The problem was, I didn't believe that I could do it, that I could become a successful, self-supporting writer. Most aspiring writers don't, and what they hear from those in the know confirms their worst suspicions: they'll never become writers, the industry is extremely competitive, it eats its young, only the well-connected survive. But this doesn't have to be true, as I (and countless other writers) have learned, once we finally started to believe in ourselves and trust in our talent and hard work.

But where do you get that kind of belief in yourself? For me, it was an unusual road. I began training in the martial arts more than ten years ago, when I was a graduate student just hoping to lose a little weight and get in shape. What I didn't expect was that learning a martial art would teach me how to succeed as a writer. But it did.

I learned to focus, and to believe in myself, and to persevere. I learned how to acquire discipline, and how to accept criticism, and how to keep going despite setbacks. All of these were lessons necessary to my eventual success as a writer.

When I finally applied what I learned in the martial arts to my writing career, my writing career took off. Within a few years, I had published an armful of books, and I was doing better financially than I ever thought possible. I attracted an agent who could help me—one who saw herself as a partner in my career. The two of us worked together to make the most of my talent, training and expertise (previous agents hadn't been successful in selling my work). I sold books to much larger publishing houses and reached a much wider, more mainstream audience.

Other writers started to ask me how I had accomplished what I had accomplished, so I branched out and began teaching writing classes, workshops and seminars. Students in my writing classes find new ways to get in touch with their creativity and say what's on their mind by following the program I set out. Writers who attend my workshops and seminars feel the lessons energize them and give control to them. They feel encouraged, not discouraged. They tell me that they receive far more interest from editors and agents than they did before learning the lessons I ask them to incorporate in their writing lives. Writers whom I coach report back to me on their successes at breaking into publishing. One writer told me that by following my advice, she wrote a book proposal that eventually sold at an eight-house auction for more than the winning bidder had ever paid for a manuscript in its forty-year history.

In other words, the lessons I learned not only work for me, but for other writers as well. And they not only make you a better writer, they can help you become more successful—so that you can give up your day job, too (but only if you want to).

In *Dojo Wisdom for Writers,* I share these lessons so that you can learn to believe in yourself. You don't have to be a martial artist to understand them, or to apply them—in fact, the great thing about the lessons is that you *don't* have to enroll in the nearest Karate school. You just have to be willing to put them into practice.

Dojo Wisdom for Writers is based on my own experiences as a writer, my experiences as a writing teacher and coach, plus the experiences of countless other writers—most of whom are not martial artists, but who have had to learn the lessons one way or another. By following these simple lessons based on martial arts wisdom, you can find success in your own writing life.

The Korean martial arts have a saying: "Pilsung!" This means "Certain Victory!" After hearing and using that word for a lot of years, I finally began to mean it whenever I shouted it. It's now my mantra, battle-cry and affirmation. If ever I get frustrated or afraid, I just tell myself, "Certain Victory!" And I achieve what I want to achieve.

If you follow the lessons in *Dojo Wisdom for Writers,* you will make your writing dreams a reality, too. You will also achieve Certain Victory. If I can do it, anyone can. *Pilsung!*

Find a teacher

In the martial arts, we have a saying: "When the student is ready, the master appears." Like the time when I felt old and out-of-shape, trying to quit smoking, and gaining weight at the rate of about three pounds a day, and I walked by a Tae Kwon Do school on my way to the liquor store. The school had always been there, of course. I just happened to need it right then and so I "saw" it for the first time. I went in and signed up and never looked back.

Every martial artist has a teacher (and sometimes more than one). That person shapes your growth as a martial artist, so it's important to find the right one—the one who will encourage and challenge you without making you feel totally inadequate.

The same is true for writers. Every writer needs a teacher. It doesn't have to be a teacher who stands in front of the class and lectures, or one who critiques your work on a regular basis. The teacher may be a novelist whose style you admire. Or it may be a book of writing instruction that connects with you. It may be an editor or an agent. If you're lucky (and you're looking), you can find teachers to help you through every stage of your writing career. In the earlier stages, it may be someone who can help you craft your work. In the middle stages, it may be someone who can help you gain access to the publishing industry. In the later stages of your career, it may be someone who can teach you how to keep your writing fresh and yourself renewed.

Writer Mary Shafer encourages writers to find "as broad a spectrum of teachers as you can find." She challenges writers to find teachers who don't share their worldview—the more uncomfortable you are, the more you will be challenged, and the more you will be forced to clarify your thoughts and become a more effective thinker. "Also," she says, "this makes you a less gullible researcher." She cautions writers not to accept just anyone, and not to be fooled by the glitter of celebrity and fame. "Really good teachers are usually too busy to be famous, except among those who have benefited from their wisdom," Mary says.

Exercise

Consider who in your life right now might be a good teacher for you as a writer. If you have someone in mind, consider yourself an apprentice. It doesn't need to be a formal relationship. You could offer to buy the teacher lunch if he or she will give you some pointers about writing.

If no one pops to mind, then keep yourself open to finding a teacher. Don't force the issue, but do pursue opportunities that you may have disregarded before. For example, take a writing class at a nearby college or arts center. Attend a writers' workshop. Join a writers' organization and participate in local meetings. Go online and take part in writers' listservs and bulletin boards. Hit the library and find books by writers you admire, and books about writing that can guide you. Let others around you know that you're open to finding a teacher or mentor who can help you shape your writing and your writing career.

2
Trust your teacher

When a student begins training in the martial arts, he doesn't know what to expect or what will be required of him. He has to trust his teacher. He has to trust that his teacher won't exploit him or take advantage of his inexperience; he has to trust that his teacher will give him the information he needs to know; he has to trust that when the teacher says, "You can do this," he can do this.

Most of us who train never believed it possible to do the things we now do. But we trusted the teacher who told us we could do it if we would just try. And the teacher was right.

Debz Buller, one of my martial arts students who has also become a writer, didn't believe she could do it the first time I told her she was ready to break a board with a sidekick. But I had a lot more experience with people breaking boards with sidekicks than she did, so I knew what I was talking about. I knew she was ready. She took a deep breath and decided to trust me. She let out a yell and kicked and broke the board. I'll never forget the grin that lit up her whole face. I could actually see her self-confidence zoom up the scale. Suddenly, she knew she could take on an attacker. She knew she could do anything. I could just see her thinking, "Watch out, world!"

Months later, she mentioned that she had always wanted to become a writer. This time, when I told her I thought she was ready, she trusted me. The result is that she is a published author. If she hadn't trusted me, she might still be listening to the self-doubts that told her she couldn't do it.

As in martial arts, the writer has to trust (while using some judgment). In other words, when an agent answers your query letter by saying, "I think I can sell your book if you give me $3,000 to edit it," some caution is prudent. But when an agent answers your query letter by saying, "This query would be more effective if you approached the project from a different point of view," maybe you should think about approaching the project from a different point of view.

Begin with small things and if the teacher proves trustworthy in those small things, be willing to take greater risks and trust the teacher with more important and larger things. For example, when my current agent contacted me, she said she was looking for a martial arts expert to write an introductory book for martial artists (this book turned out to be *Martial Arts for Dummies.*) Having been in the business for a while, I was cautious. I asked her for information about herself—her clients and books sold. She asked for a bio from me. Later, she came back and said the editor wanted me to provide a table of contents for my vision of the book; and she, the agent, wanted me to sign a letter of agreement with her. Again, being cautious, I asked if the editor would call me first. The agent arranged this. I spoke with the editor, was reassured that everyone involved was serious, and so I provided the table of contents and signed the letter of agreement which was for this one book only.

This series of steps all entailed very small risks on my

part—a few hours of my time and no long-term committments to an agent I didn't know very well. I landed the contract, the agent negotiated the deal and everyone was happy. Next, my agent asked me if I had other projects in mind. I explained an idea I had for a book about how training in the martial arts had changed people's lives. She suggested I think about putting the book together in a series of short, simple lessons. I wasn't sure that I wanted to do that—it wasn't exactly what I had envisioned. But so far she had been right about everything she had told me. So I trusted that she knew about the business. I did as she asked—and the result was the *Dojo Wisdom* series. This teacher has earned my trust and I listen very closely to her suggestions, ideas and advice, even when I'm not sure I can do what she thinks I can.

Exercise

The next time a teacher in your life (one who knows you're a writer) says to you, "Why don't you do . . . X?" follow the teacher's advice—go to that writers' workshop, take a class, submit your poem to a journal. The worst risk you're taking is that you might lose some time and money, and your ego might get skinned a bit. But often the teacher knows that you're ready for the next step or the next challenge, when you're still a little unsure of yourself. Trust the teacher, follow her suggestion and be glad you did no matter what happens.

3
Respect the centerline

In the martial arts, the centerline is the source of your power—your base or your center. Centerline refers to an imaginary line that starts between your eyes and goes down to the ground, dividing your body in half. By focusing on protecting your centerline, you make yourself less vulnerable to serious attack. In other words, you protect your face, throat, chest and abdomen from crippling attacks, and instead use the less vulnerable parts of your anatomy (your limbs) to attack, defend and block. An injury to your arm or foot is much less damaging to you than an injury to your internal organs.

For writers, respecting the centerline means keeping your writing and your self-esteem safe. You need to protect your writing in a conscious way. That means finding time for it and not letting other problems or demands take you away from it. It means believing in yourself even when other people have a negative opinion of you or your writing.

Many writers, for example, pay as little attention to reviews as possible. Reviews may be important to sell books, but a review is just one person's opinion. Giving a review (especially a negative one) too much weight can cripple you as a writer. In the same way, allowing negative people to attack your writing and your writing goals can cripple you. If someone important in your life cannot be supportive of your writing goals, protect yourself and your goals from that person. Don't give in to the negative. Protect and respect your centerline.

Finally, remember that the term "centerline" derives from the idea of "center." If writing is indeed your center, it must be protected and nurtured at all costs.

Exercise

Connect with other writers on a regular basis. It should go without saying that these writers should be supportive, encouraging writers, not ones who'll constantly whine about the state of the industry and tell you not to quit your day job. Get involved in a writing community that will help you understand what you could be doing better, and that will help you understand what makes writers succeed. If the community turns out to be negative or hypercritical, leave. Find a new community.

Take some time when choosing a community before becoming too involved so that you can make sure it will suit your needs. But once you're sure that it does, immerse yourself in it and get what you can from it (giving a little is also good).

Sometimes the "community" can be one other writer you meet for lunch or coffee once a week or once a month. Don't discount these meetings. They can be an excellent way to respect your centerline.

4
From your Chi flows your creativity

Chi (also qi and ki) is the inner energy each of us possesses, the life force that permeates the universe. Martial artists learn to tap into this energy in order to focus their efforts and reach the goals they want to achieve. The shout, called the *kiai* or *kihop,* that martial artists use as they strike is a physical summoning of the Chi. It helps the martial artist concentrate on what needs to be done (striking the opponent, breaking the board, surviving the promotion test.) A martial artist learns that she can do anything if she taps into and summons her Chi. But you have a limited amount of Chi at any given time. If you constantly draw on your Chi without renewing it, you can feel depleted and down.

For a writer, Chi is the source of creativity. If you spend all your time working a day job and then expect to come home at night and work on your writing, you may find your creative energies are low and you can't think of anything to write. Sometimes a schedule change can make all the difference. Instead of trying to write after a ten-hour day at the office, set aside time on the weekends and protect that time.

The amount of Chi or life energy you have to spend in any given day is limited. Many writers are faced with many competing demands: you have to work, and raise your kids and provide brownies for the school fundraiser while trying to carve out some time to write. Instead of feeling calm and balanced, you may feel overwhelmed and empty. You use up your life energy on everything but writing. Often, the stress makes you feel frustrated, discontented and even angry—and those emotions make it even more difficult to write.

Creativity feeds on Chi, which requires, rest, balance and peace.

Exercise

Cultivate your creative energy. Remember that like any energy it needs fuel and rest to recharge. Create an environment where you can recharge your Chi. Set aside space and time to reflect and to renew yourself. Empty, unscheduled time can help you feel less rushed and can give your Chi a chance to rejuvenate.

Gain control over that stressed-out feeling. Give up all of those crazy expectations you have for yourself and your life and focus only on those expectations that matter most to you. A long time ago, I gave up having the spotless house that I used to feel was very important. I try to wash the dishes before any mold actually grows on them, but if the carpet doesn't get vacuumed this week, it doesn't matter to me. You can give up some of the time-consuming things you do in order to have more Chi for your writing.

Guard your writing energy by making writing a priority in your life. Develop a ritual you can use to re-energize. Maybe it's a cup of soothing tea before you sit at your desk, or a few minutes in the tub, soaking the cares of the day away. Give your creative energy nourishment.

5
Meditate

Martial artists meditate for many reasons. They meditate to empty their minds and achieve *aiki,* or impassive mind (see *Lesson #29:* Aiki, *the impassive mind, brings strength*), which helps them respond to threats and challenges in a logical, rational way, unclouded by fear and doubt. Martial artists also use meditation to contemplate aspects of the martial arts in the hopes of achieving a deeper understanding of them. They also use visualization, a type of meditation that helps them "see" how they can perform their techniques perfectly. They often use this type of meditation shortly before a challenge—such as a promotion test or a tournament sparring match. Some martial artists also meditate to reach enlightenment, the way a Zen Buddhist does. Many also perform physical meditation, where they do a physical activity such as walking (or martial arts forms or techniques) where they focus only on the physical effort and not on any thoughts, in an attempt to calm and renew the mind.

For a writer, meditation can be an extremely useful tool. A writer, like a martial artist, can meditate to clear his or her mind before starting an evening's work. This allows the time set aside for writing to be used for writing instead of worrying about the nineteen other things left undone that day. As author Miryam Williamson says, "With the ability to empty the mind comes the ability to focus it."

Writers also use meditation as a means to visualize the

successful completion of their work. They envision themselves overcoming challenges and obstacles. They may visualize themselves receiving a phone call accepting their latest work for publication, and this visualization inspires them to sit down and write even if they're tired and feel like all they'll ever get is rejection letters. They may visualize their characters in different settings, eventually visualizing an entire plot. Writers can also spend time in contemplation—considering how best to achieve the effects they want in their writing, going below the surface to understand their true purpose in writing. It's even possible that a writer or two has achieved enlightenment through meditation, although I make no promises.

E x e r c i s e

Add a few minutes of meditation to your daily routine. Try fitting it in shortly before you begin your daily writing session. Begin practicing a simple version of *zazen* (mind-emptying) meditation, until you feel comfortable that you've got it down. To do this, find a quiet spot where you won't be interrupted for at least ten or fifteen minutes. Find a comfortable place to sit, such as a cushion on the floor. Dim the lights so they're not glaring as you're trying to relax. After you're comfortable, close your eyes. Take several deep breaths and focus on relaxing your body. Then focus on a single image in your mind. (I use a candle flame but it can be anything—something neutral and not distracting is best.) Just look at that image in your mind. Don't think anything about the image. Just look at it. When thoughts wander in, firmly reject them and focus on the image. It takes some practice to learn to do this, but it comes eventually.

Once you become familiar with what you can achieve

through zazen meditation, you can practice other types. If you're suffering a lot of doubts about your writing, for example, choose visualization, where you see yourself succeeding as a writer. I accept the Pulitzer Prize whenever I'm feeling down about my work, and that inspires me to keep plugging along. You can find a vision that helps inspire you, too.

6

Be open to what happens next

A martial artist doesn't decide how a sparring match will go ahead of time. Instead, he lets the match flow. He doesn't worry about what the opponent is going to do next. He knows that no matter what the opponent does, he can counter it. The opponent's strikes become tools that the martial artist uses to perform his own techniques. The opponent may punch and leave his chest wide open for a kick. The opponent may kick and leave himself open for a counter-kick. The martial artist gets into the flow of the match and responds to what happens without fear or anxiety. While he wants to control the match, he doesn't telegraph his moves or disregard the opponent's moves. He remains open and balanced.

The writer who is open to what happens next can use the experience to build on, just as the martial artist does. Even a negative experience can yield something positive for the writer. One such experience stands out for me. A publisher canceled a book contract after I had finished exhaustively researching and writing an encyclopedia of the

Middle Ages (I'd spent *years* on this puppy). A new managing editor wanted to take the publishing house in a different direction, and my book didn't factor in. I was allowed to keep my very meager advance and see if anyone else wanted to do the book.

So I did. No one wanted that particular book. But one publisher was interested in a book on women in the Middle Ages, so I took all the entries that had to do with women, compiled a few more, and produced *Encyclopedia of Women in the Middle Ages,* a reference book that has become a top seller for the publisher. Later, I proposed a book on the Byzantine Empire to the same publisher. I took the Byzantine entries from the original encyclopedia, buffed them up, added a few more and ended up with *Encyclopedia of the Byzantine Empire.* Instead of having one failed book and a lot of wasted time, I ended up with two published books quietly earning royalties.

Writer Jennie Schacht describes how a similar situation worked for her. As a food writer, she had the idea to write a potluck cookbook. Everyone she spoke with thought it was an excellent idea. Only one problem: she couldn't convince a publisher that it was an excellent idea. In the meantime, she took a chocolate class with a pastry chef—and "perhaps a bit cocky from a surfeit of chocolate," she says—she approached the chef and invited her to call if she ever wanted to write a book or get her thoughts into print. Jennie reports that they have co-authored an article and are now co-authoring a cookbook to be published by Chronicle Books. What about the potluck cookbook? Well, she certainly hopes it will be published, "But even if not, I was open to something different and it came along," she says.

Exercise

Although you may have a plan for your writing career, keep yourself open to opportunities as they arise, and be willing to go in another direction. Take an unexpected detour now and then. A few years ago, I joined the National Writers Union because they offered health insurance for self-employed writers. Shortly after I joined, I was urged to become a member of the representative assembly that sets guidelines and procedures for the union. Feeling a little bored that day, I nominated myself and was elected (everyone who nominated themselves was elected.) At the assembly, I met dozens of other writers who had triumphs and challenges just like mine. After working so many years in isolation, this was a breath of fresh air for me. One of the people I met suggested I run for co-chair of the Book Division. After about two minutes of thought, I said okay, and by the end of the weekend I had been elected. I plunged into a brand-new world. Suddenly, dozens of writers were coming to me for answers to their questions about the publishing industry. I was asked to speak at seminars and workshops. A whole new direction opened up for me—coaching writers in addition to coaching martial artists. Eventually, this new direction led to the book you're now reading. Being open to what happens next has added a new layer to my career and has renewed my energy and enthusiasm for writing. If you can be open to these new experiences, you'll find your energy and enthusiasm for writing being constantly renewed as well.

7

Respect your opponent

A wise martial artist does not judge the opponent based on appearances only. She respects her opponent. She respects the possibility that her opponent could challenge her and be difficult to defeat, even if the opponent doesn't appear daunting at first.

As a martial artist, you don't always know what hidden strengths or techniques an opponent may have. Respecting your opponent means you don't sell him short or make quick judgments. It means respecting the warrior aspect of your opponent, even if he does not measure up to you in the sparring ring.

In writing, your "opponent" may appear in different guises. It may be another writer who is competing with you for the same assignments and the same publishing opportunities. It may be a book reviewer who fails to recognize your brilliance and criticizes your work in public. Many writers feel that agents and editors are "opponents"—after all, agents and editors are the gatekeepers and you have to get by them in order to achieve success as a writer. (A more fitting analogy would be to call editors and agents "judges," since they're in the position to critique your work and accept or reject it.) In other words, a writer's "opponents" are either the people with whom he is in direct competition or else the people who want him to do things differently from the way he is doing them.

In writing, dealing with these various "opponents"

means respecting them and, as author Bob Spear recommends, "Never becoming complacent and never letting your guard (your professionalism) down." If, for example, the editor makes recommendations for editing, respect the editor enough to seriously consider making the changes. The editor's fresh reading eyes may help you create an even better piece of writing than you could manage without her. If an agent rejects your proposal, suggesting that you need a stronger platform, instead of dismissing her comments out of hand, maybe you should explore the idea further.

It's also important to respect other writers, particularly those in your field. If you respect their experiences and their advice, you'll learn valuable information that can help you succeed (sometimes you learn what *not* to do). If you think other writers have nothing worthwhile to say, you'll probably find yourself making avoidable errors and running into challenges and obstacles that another writer could have given you a roadmap for getting around. Of course, it's easy to respect other writers whom you admire and whose work you enjoy reading, but it's equally important to respect other writers whose work is not necessarily to your taste or in your field. At a conference, Robert W. Walker once taught me a great deal about promoting my writing, even though he's a horror novelist and I write nonfiction books.

When my agent said, "Small books with short lessons are extremely popular. They're a great way to communicate ideas to people who might not want to dig into the longer, more narrative form you're so fond of," I was inclined to dismiss her comments. "Extremely popular" wasn't the most important thing in the world to me. But on reflection, I realized that I needed to respect her opinion. I had been looking for a strategy to connect with readers outside my usual core audience. If I could entice them by offering a simple, friendly book, arranged in an easy and accessible way, then that would be worth the effort. Thus *Dojo Wisdom* was born. By following an approach that other writers—"opponents"—had used, I was able to appeal to a much larger audience and reach one of my writing goals (to bring martial arts knowledge to non-martial artists).

Exercise

Take some time to study what other writers are doing—particularly those writers you do not ordinarily read or connect with. For example, if you're not a romance reader or writer, you may not be familiar with what's happening in the field. You may even dismiss it as not worthy of your attention. But if you respect what romance writers are doing, you may be able to emulate their success, or at least understand the market forces that make some romance authors so successful, which should tell you something. In the same way, instead of dismissing the work of that best-selling author as substandard, look at what he or she did to make the book best-selling. It may tell you something you can use in your own work and in your own book promotion.

8

Keep the beginner's mind

Martial artists respect the beginner's mind because it's open to new experiences and isn't as critical as it later becomes. Someone who is just beginning to train in the martial arts doesn't have bad habits or preconceived ideas that she must overcome before she can learn the principles the teacher communicates. As students progress and become more knowledgeable, they become less open and less flexible. They know that there's a right way and a wrong way to perform a sidekick, and they'll point out if you're doing it the wrong way.

A good martial artist eventually matures beyond this stage and returns to the beginning in the sense that she opens herself to new experiences, new techniques, new ways of performing the old kicks. She understands that there are many different, but still legitimate, ways to perform a sidekick, and while she may do it a certain way, it is not the only way, or even the best way.

By maintaining an open beginner's mind—being willing to learn and to not close yourself to new and different experiences and projects—you can achieve writing success. After more than twenty published books, I still think there must be secrets to writing and publishing that I don't know, and I want to find out what they are. So when relatively new writers share their experiences with me, I listen because I may learn something.

A writing colleague of mine reads at least one writing

book a month because even after years in the business he can often glean one idea or strategy that can make a difference in his career. Often the authors of these writing books have less experience than he does, but that doesn't stop him from "listening."

Exercise

Beginning writers naturally keep an open mind to what they learn about writing. Their beginner's mind is fully operational. The trick is to remain open even after you've achieved some success as a writer. More advanced writers are often defeated by an inner, censoring critic that says things like, "That's okay for beginners to do, but I'm much too experienced for that." For those writers, staying open means occasionally doing something "only" a beginner would do, like attending a writers' conference as an attendee and not a speaker. Or submitting work to a contest, or following a piece of advice that "never works for me" just to see what happens.

9
No knowledge is useless

While a martial artist chooses the most effective techniques for her and develops an arsenal that reflects her abilities, physical condition and typical opponent, she knows that the more knowledge she acquires, the better off she'll be. So she continually seeks out new challenges, new teachers and new techniques to hone her skills and increase her arsenal. Some of the knowledge she acquires does not seem to have a direct application to her ability to do battle. For example, she learns forms, which are patterns of movements like a dance, not because she'll ever use the form in battle but because forms teach her balance, agility and how to follow up one technique with another. And that knowledge may be extremely useful to her someday.

In writing, the same is true. You may have more research for an article than you really needed, but perhaps it will come in handy for the next article, or for a book down the road. Someone may pass on some publicity ideas that aren't relevant now because you're focusing on writing magazine articles, but which may come in handy in the future when you turn those magazine articles into a book.

For fiction writers, "useless" knowledge can add dimension to characters and plots, making them seem real. John Grisham uses his understanding of the law and lawyers to write his thrillers. When he chose to become a writer, he could have decided that all the time he spent studying the law was "useless" but instead he turned it to his advantage to create plots and situations that seem plausible because of his special, detailed knowledge of the field. Best-selling author Barbara Michaels (who also writes under the name Elizabeth Peters) uses her background as an archaelogist to enhance her Amelia Peabody mysteries. Reading her books, you get a sense that any subject that interests her (country music, romance novels, Richard III) eventually becomes part of a novel. She obviously indulges her interest in a wide-range of subjects and finds ways to work her "useless" knowledge into her plots and characterizations.

Mary Higgins Clark cuts out newspaper articles that spark her ideas and uses them as she envisions the main characters and plot points in her books.

E x e r c i s e

A lot of that so-called "useless knowledge" takes the form of paper—notes from an interview, research you no longer need for an article, resources someone has passed along to you, photocopies of an article that enraged you and made you want to take action. Your inner neatnik may encourage you to toss it, but that information may be gold someday, whether you're a fiction or a nonfiction writer. Having the exact details available deepens your prose (and also your poetry). It can become a jumping off point for your fiction ("What if my protagonist were a scuba diver like the one profiled in last week's newspaper?") or a source of specific facts and information for your nonfiction.

So instead of tossing it, set up a filing system whereby you can easily retrieve information you may need someday in your work. You don't need to be a packrat about it—a two-drawer filing cabinet is sufficient for most writers, and it can go in the back of a closet somewhere. Don't save basic information that you can get anywhere, anytime, just by using the dictionary or the local yellow pages. Instead, save esoteric information, stories in the newspaper that intrigued you, and resources—that is, the experts, websites and books you can turn to in order to find the statistics you need or the quote you have to have.

10

Perseverance brings rewards

No one gets the spinning wheel kick right the first time they try it. They don't get the shoulder drop throw, or chon-ji form, either. It takes persistence and perseverance to learn the techniques of the martial arts. It takes repeated practice, and an awful lot of bruised shins. But this perseverance eventually brings rewards: a technique mastered, a board broken, a sparring match won, a black belt earned— and the ultimate prize, the confidence that you can take care of yourself.

Likewise, perseverance is the most important trait a writer can have. It's even more important than talent. As medical writer Miryam Williamson, the author of several health books, points out, "The only mistake you can make with a manuscript you believed in enough to write it is to give up on it."

Author Randy Peyser says that to get published, "I had to be the pitbull of perseverance. It took me seven years from the time I wrote my book to the time it came out in print." She explains that at one point she worked for a magazine that didn't pay her for six months. When the magazine folded, leaving her with an empty bank account, she knew she had to get creative fast. "So I put together a one-woman show in which I read parts of my manuscript, played drums and guitar and added some comedy," she says, which helped pay the bills. This also helped out in another way: "The next time I went to Book Expo America, I discovered that publishers were interested in me because of the show. That was what gave me a national platform. I snagged a contract within two weeks of the BEA. Now my book's a best-seller for the publisher!"

II

Flexibility is strength

Martial artists train to get the most power into their throws, kicks and punches. To do this, they build muscle, often by lifting weights or by going through endurance training that otherwise intelligent people should have the sense to avoid. This makes them strong (and maybe a little sore).

But they also work on flexibility and agility. They stretch their muscles during every training session so that they can kick higher or throw more easily. If they don't balance the muscle-building with flexibility-training, they'll have bulging biceps but they won't be able to bend over to pick up the car keys they just dropped. If they had to defend themselves, they'd only be able to kick the attacker's ankle. While this *can* be an effective self-defense technique, it's no substitute for being able to kick someone in the groin.

So one of the lessons the martial artist learns is that flexibility is strength. She learns this in a physical way—by physically stretching her muscles and tendons and ligaments. She also learns that if she can be flexible mentally, she'll be more successful as a martial artist. If her favorite kick is a roundhouse kick, but today's sparring partner keeps blocking the roundhouse kick, she needs to be flexible enough, mentally, to switch gears and try a different technique. This doesn't mean her roundhouse kick isn't a good roundhouse kick. It just means that sometimes the roundhouse kick isn't the best technique for the opponent she's facing. If she can switch to a different technique, she has a much better chance of winning the match (or defending herself against the attacker).

How does this apply to the writing life? Writers also need to cultivate flexibility in order to succeed. A writer unwilling to change her tactics won't do as well as one who will. Remember, the path to success (whatever success means to you) is different for everyone. If you talk to five writers who have been published, you'll hear five different stories about how they got their foot in the door and convinced an editor to take on their first story or article or book.

If there's no one way to get where you want to go, then you need to be willing to try alternate routes. If one approach isn't working for you, it doesn't mean you have to abandon all hopes for writing success. Maybe you just need to try a different approach. If you've been sending out five query letters a week for the last two years with no nibbles, maybe you should try going to writers' conferences to meet editors and agents and learn their needs. Maybe you need to take a writing class at a nearby college. Maybe you should find out if Erica Jong needs an apprentice.

Being flexible pays off in ways you may not expect. When I was very young, I knew I wanted to be a writer. I also knew that I wanted to be a novelist. I wrote my first novel when I was eleven. But no one wanted to publish my fiction. I kept trying, although by the time I was in my mid-twenties, I was trying less hard. But when I began training in martial arts, I began looking at my writing differently. I saw that I could be more flexible. Sure, I had always wanted to be a novelist. But was that the only way to be a writer? I decided that more than anything I wanted to be a writer. It didn't matter what kind.

I investigated a little further and learned that it's easier to get nonfiction published than it is to get fiction published. So I wrote a proposal about a book on country music (which I love). I found a publisher within two months. Next, I wondered what else I could write about. I realized that I loved martial arts, and that most martial arts writing was . . . err . . . terrible. Surely someone would snap up martial arts writing by a person who could string together an entire paragraph without making six grammatical errors? So I proposed an encyclopedia of martial arts. Again, the proposal sold within two months. I was on my way.

Little did I know that I would end up the Queen of Martial Arts writing. It wasn't quite where I intended to go when I started out, but it combines two of my passions in one career. Had I insisted on writing only novels, I would probably still be unpublished today, teaching classes at the local community college instead of pursuing the career I've always dreamed of having. Now, I'm doing what I've always wanted to do. Just a little differently than I expected.

Exercise

Ask yourself what preconceptions you have about writing, being a writer, and living the writing life. Are any of these preconceptions getting in the way of your success? Can you be more flexible in your definition of "writing," "being a writer," and "living the writing life"? If you're a poet, can you write magazine articles to supplement your addiction? I once spent a summer writing greeting card sentiments so I could spend an autumn writing a dark, terribly moving novel that no one wanted to publish. I'm proud of both projects. If you feel that writing brochures for the travel agency down the street would be selling out, ask yourself how working as a claims adjuster for the insurance agency is *not* selling out. We often worry about keeping our writing "pure," when if we would look at it from another angle, we would see that we're limiting our chances for success.

12

A warrior masters many techniques

A martial artist soon learns that if he relies only on his two favorite techniques, an opponent will quickly find a way around those two techniques and defeat him. A good fighter may like using hand techniques and find them very effective, but he also trains in foot techniques, recognizing that there may come a time when he can't use his hands (because he's carrying a child, because his arm is broken, because both hands are tied behind his back). He may prefer not to rely on weapons but will train in their use anyway so that when he's facing a weapon, it won't unnecessarily frighten or confuse him, and because in a certain situation he may want to grab an object in the environment (i.e, a baseball bat) and use it as a weapon. In other words, a warrior masters many techniques, knowing he may need them.

Writer and artist Samantha Clark, an organizer for the National Writers Union, has had to put this principle into action in her life. An accomplished artist who won a scholarship to a top art school, she developed carpal tunnel syndrome in her hands when she was in her early twenties. "Suddenly," she says, "I became an unskilled worker with student loans to repay and not much of a career future. I had always pictured myself spending my time completely immersed in my art." She relates how she met a Plains Indian medicine woman who "told me the reason my hands became disabled was that I had *more important* things to do in life." Samantha doesn't know if the medicine woman told her that just to make her feel better, but no matter what, it worked. She started writing as a new outlet for her creativity. And, she says, "Several years after my injury I found some new art forms like printmaking and photography. My hands aren't any better. I'll never get that lost talent back. But I've learned that life is a series of opportunities if I can ignore my preconceived ideas and just live in the moment." Samantha has learned that she doesn't have to give up being a creative person just because one creative outlet is denied to her.

Writing is one form of creativity. It can be enhanced and complimented by mastering other forms of creativity. In the same way that you shouldn't confine yourself to just one mode of writing (poetry only or nonfiction only), you shouldn't confine yourself to just the designation "writer." Maybe you can also be a photographer or a producer or a graphic artist.

Try learning a technique that may be related to writing but is not writing. Maybe it's marketing or maybe it's learning to draw. Either one can enhance your success as a writer. Think more imaginatively about your creativity and you'll find that you blossom as a writer.

13

Discipline leads to strength

A martial artist practices discipline to become stronger. By disciplining herself to learn the techniques of her art even when she'd rather be doing something else, she becomes stronger—able to defend herself in ways she could not before. By training even when she doesn't feel like training, she builds strength and endurance in her body. She learns that by having discipline in related areas—such as the diet she eats—she becomes fitter and more able to master the martial art she studies, and thus becomes stronger. She learns to discipline her emotions—anger, frustration, fear—

as she steps into the sparring ring, and that brings her emotional strength in the match.

The writer also needs discipline to become strong. Writer Mary Shafer says this is probably the most difficult thing a writer must learn. "Without the discipline to apply butt to seat and pound out those words, writing just doesn't happen," she says. "Developing the discipline to produce, to research but know when to stop looking things up and writing them down, to respect and meet deadlines—all these are critical to developing the strength of our craft."

Discipline may also be needed in other ways—to rewrite a piece that needs it even when you don't feel like it, to start over again and draft the novel from the beginning when it runs into unfixable problems in the middle, to dump the gorgeous phrases that don't otherwise fit the tone of your story. But learning to develop discipline will help you master the craft and ultimately lead to success in writing.

In an interview with *Writer's Digest*, Pulitzer Prize–winning best-selling author Michael Chabon says, "There are three things that are required for success as a writer: talent, luck, discipline. It can be in any combination, but there's nothing you do to influence the first two. Discipline is the one element . . . that you can control, and so that is the one that you have to focus on." He concludes: "Keep a regular schedule and write at the same time every day for the same amount of time. That's it. That is the sum total of my wisdom."

Exercise

If there is some area of your writing life that needs discipline—for example, you never seem to find the time to write, or you never seem to meet a deadline, or you never quite get that short story done—discipline yourself to achieve it. Set aside an hour every evening for writing if you can never find time to write, or schedule an appointment for yourself every weekend. Make whatever arrangements are necessary—tape your favorite television show, make the kids do the dishes, go to the corner coffee shop to get some peace—and then simply make it your habit to write for that block of time. Even if you think you're writing gibberish, you're getting into the habit of using discipline to achieve your goals.

14

Know your target

A martial artist must know what he is trying to achieve with every technique. When he trains, he doesn't just slice the sword through the air, but he practices against a target so that his aim is true. When he delivers a kick, he knows whether he's aiming for the knee or the groin. He knows what he hopes to accomplish with a specific fight or a specific battle—he knows what his objective is. In a sparring match, it might be to score more points than the opposing fighter. It might be to pin the opponent to the match. It might be to knock the opponent out. The martial artist also knows the vulnerable points or weak spots on an opponent's body. The martial artist always considers his target as he trains.

The writer must be the same way. You must understand what you're trying to do and what you hope to accomplish. Author Bob Spear puts it this way: "Know who you're writing for. Know what they like and don't like." In other words, if you're writing for an audience of mystery fans, your novel should have some mystery in it. If you're writing nonfiction, you need to know what your audience wants from your article or book. If your audience is young adults, you'll use different language than you would for older adults. If your audience is technically proficient in the subject matter, you'd probably use more jargon than if you were writing an introductory piece for people with no background in the subject matter. In short, you must know your target to write effectively.

Exercise

For the next piece of writing you do, create a profile of your target. To whom will you be writing? Don't go with the vague, anonymous, "general adult reader." What are their specific characteristics? Will your readers be men or women, adults or children? What are their ages? If they're adults, are they married, single, divorced? Do they have children? What ages are their children? What are their interests and hobbies? Where will you find them?

This profile can be extremely difficult for beginning writers to envision, but since the target shapes your writing, it's important to have clear, precise knowledge of the target. Having created this profile, you can then use it as a guide to reaching the audience. You can use techniques that show the audience you know their problems and concerns and that you identify with them. If you're writing a magazine article on health care, and you know that your target audience is married women with children, you can connect with them by mentioning your own husband and daughter and your concerns about their health.

Having this specific audience in mind also helps you write to them in a way they will find meaningful and accessible.

15

Teach others and you will learn

When a martial artist has achieved a certain level of competency in her martial art, she begins to teach it—and discovers that this is where the true learning begins. To demonstrate the techniques and coach other students, the martial artist must become intimately familiar with the mechanics of each technique, why it's done, and why it's done the way it's done. To keep ahead of her students, the teacher must always strive to learn more. When she's asked a tough question, she may say, "I don't know," but then she'll feel compelled to find out.

Her students also bring information and challenges to her that she learns and grows from. To become a good teacher, she must discover more patience than she thought possible. She will have to demand more of herself so that she doesn't hold her students back. And she must think on her feet constantly and creatively.

The writer must do the same. Sharing her experiences with other writers is not simply a generous impulse but also a way for her to continue to master the craft. Maggie Frisch, editor and publisher of *Working Writer* newsletter, says, "I've felt proud and honored to be the editor/publisher of a newsletter that 'teaches' writing through shared knowledge, experiences, tips. But the humbling truth is that I've learned more from the readers and contributors than they could possibly learn from me. I've become much more the student than the teacher."

Taking on the role of the teacher can result in even greater mastery of craft.

Exercise

Find an opportunity to become a teacher. Think about starting a writers' group where all the members can benefit from shared information—everyone can teach and everyone can learn. If actually starting a writing group is too much to take on, at least join a critique group or a writers' organization. Learn about teaching opportunities at the local arts center, parks and recreation program, or community college writing program. Consider working with children in elementary and high school. Most public schools have programs that allow community members to come into the school to share their work and life experiences. Volunteer to be a storyteller at the local library and encourage the children who attend to write their own stories. As the teacher, you'll learn more than you thought possible about the art and craft of writing.

16

Physical strength creates mental and emotional strength

The martial artist knows that physical training helps him avoid the sword thrust that could end it all. But he also knows that any battle requires mental and emotional strength, not just physical strength. Further, the warrior recognizes that physical training helps him develop mental and emotional strength. If he trains hard and pushes himself past his physical limits, he learns not to give in to that little voice in his head saying, *Oh, this is hard. Just give up now.* He learns that he can ignore that little voice even when he isn't in physical training but when he's doing something mentally or emotionally difficult, like dealing with a serious illness or seeking marriage counseling. Instead of yielding to the *Oh, this is hard. Just give up now* voice, he develops enough mental and emotional strength to see him through the tough times.

In a more prosaic way, being physically strong makes him feel better mentally and emotionally. If he has had a good training session, he's more apt to feel upbeat and positive. Having worked on his physical skills, he's not likely to engage in a lot of negative self-defeating self-talk. This creates mental and emotional balance and strength that can help him achieve far beyond his physical goals.

The writer will also find that physical strength creates mental and emotional strength. Author Miryam Williamson says, "When I'm working on a book, I treat myself like an athlete in training: the best (in the sense of purest, least adulterated and most whole) foods I can afford, plenty of physical exercise (first thing in the morning, before I have time to think about whether I feel like it or not), regular hours for sleeping and waking so that I can get the most restorative sleep possible, and tenderness with my spiritual/emotional being." This regimen helps Miryam keep her work flowing smoothly and without interruption.

Linda Formichelli, the prolific author of more than one hundred magazine articles, who is also a Karate student, says, "Since I started studying Karate, my writing business has improved. Exercise helps me stay calm in a crisis—and believe me, there are a lot of crises when it comes to writing, from periods where I have no work to editors who change their minds more often than they change their underwear." She also feels she concentrates better and works faster when she is exercising regularly, "which means that I now work only twenty hours a week but still manage to get my assignments done on time." Thus, physical strength has helped her create mental and emotional strength, resulting in a successful writing career and a well-balanced life.

Exercise

This lesson's exercise is—you guessed it—to get some exercise. While it may be a little much to ask, especially since a lot of people don't have time to sleep, let alone pursue their writing goals *and* get some exercise, it's essential to your continued writing success that you be as physically strong as you can. If you can't see how you can fit in that daily hour at the gym, start small: treat yourself like an athlete in training and improve your eating habits.

Start parking farther from the entrance to the grocery store. Take up a sport (volleyball) or physically active hobby (gardening) that you've thought about but never had the impetus to do before. You'll be glad you did.

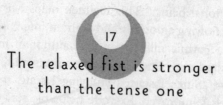

17

The relaxed fist is stronger than the tense one

Often, beginning martial artists don't quite understand how to be more "powerful." (Most of them think it's pretty good progress when they can do a kick without falling over.) The instructor will bark, "More power in your punches!" and they'll scratch their heads a bit, and then tighten their muscles as hard as they can and hit the bag. They may think they're more powerful when they do this, but they're not. Over time, they learn to turn their bodies into the punch so that the entire mass of their bodies goes into the punch, not just the mass of their arms. This helps, but it's not all they need to learn.

Mass itself does not create power. Physics tells us that "mass times acceleration equals force." So power ("force") is a combination of speed ("acceleration") and muscle mass. If you tighten your muscles as hard as you can, you're restricting your speed. You cannot hit a punching bag (or an attacker, for that matter) very quickly with tense muscles. In fact, you have to be relaxed when you perform a punch (or a kick or a throw). To do the most damage, you keep your muscles relaxed until the very moment of impact, at which time you tighten your muscles to prevent your joints from rolling.

Frequently, I instruct beginners to hit a target (like a heavy bag) to demonstrate this difference to them. They're always surprised to learn that the tense punch pushes against the bag with little power, compared to the relaxed punch, which snaps into the bag and whips it back. They usually have to try it ten times before they believe it's true.

Keeping your muscles tense the whole time you're punching makes you very tired. You can't throw as many punches. If you keep your muscles relaxed, though, you have more endurance and can throw more punches—and more powerful punches. This endurance can be the difference between winning a fight and losing it.

The act of writing often involves tension. You have only an hour to write this evening, so you better make the most of it. You have a deadline tomorrow, and if inspiration doesn't strike soon, that client will never hire you again. You look at the blank piece of paper or the glowing computer screen, and you can't think what to write. The first sentence you produce is so asinine you should probably give up and become a truck driver instead. This tension—this tightening of your writing muscles—blocks you from being able to write as effectively and successfully as possible. The more it churns your stomach to approach a writing task, the less likely you'll be able to do it well.

If, however, you can approach your writing with a more relaxed attitude, you'll be more successful at it—and you'll enjoy it more. To be more relaxed, though, you need to understand where this tension comes from. Often, it's a combination of both under- *and* overestimating how much you can accomplish in a given time. For instance, you may think it will only take a couple of hours to polish that essay when it may take a whole day. You may think it will take just a few minutes to write a query and send it along—but it takes two or three hours instead. At the same time, you may think, "I only have an hour this evening; it's not worth getting the manuscript out." But an hour can give you time to block out the next scene, or get started researching Civil War dress for your next blockbuster novel. An hour is enough to write a page or two of your book proposal.

Tension also comes from having abnormally high expectations of your work, complicated by the fact that most people don't have as much time to write as they would like. So the pressure is on to produce golden prose on your first try, in that hour you have set aside for writing this evening.

Some people are capable of producing first drafts so fabulous they don't even need to bother re-reading them before sending them off to an editor and collecting their royalty checks, but this category does not include most writers. It certainly does not include me. My first drafts are so abysmal I keep them around for laughs. I show them to my writing students, asking, "Can you write worse than this?" Anne Lamott writes about "shitty first drafts," in *Bird by Bird,* and says, "All good writers write them."

So relax about the words coming out of your pen, especially on the first draft. Just let them come out. Don't censor them before they see the light of day. Once they're down on the paper, you'll see they're not so bad. You'll also see that you can do something with them to make them better.

Exercise

Take a moment to deliberately relax the next time you sit down to write. If you're relaxed when you approach your writing, you'll feel more confident about it. You'll enjoy it more. And you'll get greater rewards from it. I can always tell when I've written something under stress—when I've tightened my writing muscles. It shows. The writing seems choppy and the ideas don't flow logically from one point to the next. It reads as if I were dragged kicking and screaming to the keyboard. To prevent this, I always consciously make myself relax before I hit the keyboard, even if I'm working under a tight deadline, or if I'm convinced I don't have a single sensible sentence in me today. I follow the same ritual each time: I turn on the computer and move everything out of sight except for what I need to work on. This helps me pretend that the only thing in the world I have to do is this particular project in front of me. I make sure all the necessary materials are assembled—reference books, interview notes and the like—so I don't have to interrupt myself and go scrabbling in the file cabinet looking for the information I know I have. I make a cup of tea and do a few deep breathing exercises. I don't look at a clock. (If I must not be late for an appointment, I set an alarm and forget about it.)

The next time you go to sit at your desk and write, and you feel that familiar tension in your shoulders, stop. Ask yourself what is causing the tension. If you're afraid you won't get the project done on deadline, ask yourself if you're being realistic. If you cannot possibly under any circumstances get the project done on time, then you need to face up to it and call the editor or client and ask for an extension. But usually this tension is unnecessary. As long as you sit down and do the assignment, you'll get it done by deadline. Tension comes from fear, often fear of the unknown. So ask yourself what is the worst thing that will happen. In this case, the worst thing is, you'll miss the deadline. Well, it ain't pretty but you won't be the first writer to miss a deadline. However, if you make yourself so anxious you can't write, not only will you miss the deadline, but you'll miss it by a month instead of by three hours. Take the attitude: So what? So what if you miss the deadline? Does that mean you'll never be allowed to write again? Of course not. (This is not to say that you should tell clients and editors, "So what?" when they call to say your copy is late. It's just a little exercise you can use to change your thought patterns so you can move beyond the fear and tension.)

Purposefully relax. Do some stretching exercises. Do a little deep breathing. Meditate if you have to. Visualize a successful writing time. Light a candle or some incense. Give yourself permission to write fifteen totally stupid sentences. Do whatever it takes to relax those muscles. If it takes a bottle of wine, fine. If you have to hide the stacks of paper needing your attention, stick 'em in the garage. A pound of chocolates? Good investment.

18

Understand what is expected of you

When a martial artist begins training, he doesn't always know what to expect. While he may have some vague idea of what he will learn, he has no clear sense of what he'll be expected to do. But if he doesn't learn pretty quickly what's expected of him, he won't succeed as a martial artist.

Many of the expectations in martial arts training are

unwritten. You may not necessarily be told you must work your hardest at all times or don't bother coming back. You may not be told that when the teacher enters the room, you're expected to rise and bow. You may not be told these things, but that's no reason not to understand them. In other words, you can learn without being told. You can observe and ask those around you. You can take responsibility for finding out what you need to know.

By learning to understand these unstated expectations, the martial artist becomes a better martial artist—because he learns to pay more attention to his surroundings, he relies on his observation skills, he learns to watch the environment even while doing another task. All of these skills make the warrior powerful.

The writer must also know what's expected of him. If you don't know what you're supposed to do, find out. Otherwise, you won't be successful as a writer. Author Miryam Williamson says, "When I accept an assignment, I spend some time interviewing the assigning editor, trying to get into her/his fantasy of what the completed work will be like. Then I try to give something a little better than was expected. This is the secret of repeat business, which is the secret of success as a freelance writer."

Exercise

If you're a beginning writer, get to know the "rules." Check out a market guide like *Writer's Market* and any of dozens of good books on the subjects of copywriting, business writing, writing novels and writing nonfiction books and magazine articles. You can sometimes break the rules, but you have to understand what they are first (sort of like grammar). Once you know what's expected of you in terms of first contact with an editor, the craft of writing, the submission of a novel or book of poems, you can be more confident of your work. At least you won't be receiving rejections for superficial and easily correctable problems like printing your manuscript on pink copy paper.

If you're a more advanced writer, raise the bar. Spend extra time finding out what's expected of you. If you get an assignment for a magazine article, make sure you've studied the magazine for audience, tone and content before drafting your piece.

19

Courtesy reveals your strength

Following the martial arts is a way of life rather than a way of war. Each martial art is a system for becoming a better person rather than just a better warrior. Many martial arts instructors set guidelines that practitioners follow to develop their characters and become better people through training. In almost all martial arts, courtesy holds a prominent position. While courtesy has to do with sportsmanship, it goes far beyond the confines of the playing field. However, sportsmanship is a good place to start. A martial artist bows to his opponent and the judges as he steps into the ring to show his respect for the opponent, the judges and the martial art. The beginning student bows to senior students and the instructor as a sign of respect for their rank. The martial artist who can show respect for others through courtesy reveals his strength. He doesn't have to play games or stroke his own ego. He is strong enough to give others their due without feeling diminished by the act.

In the same way, writers should cultivate a spirit of courtesy. I've had my moments where the prima donna in me has leaked out, and I have always regretted it afterward. I realize that if I had been courteous, I could have avoided a conflict or kept a client. I once got hard-nosed about a long-term client who was changing direction on a project I was involved in. For many years, I had written teacher's guides and supplemental material for this client at a good hourly rate. During one project, they asked me to do some Internet research. Partway through, they decided to bring that part of the project in-house. They promised they would get in touch with me for the next stage of the project. Feeling insulted (didn't they think I could research on the Internet, for goodness' sake?), I demanded to get paid for the work I had done and even mentioned my lawyer in a letter I enclosed with my invoice. They didn't indicate that they *weren't* going to pay me for my time; I was just upset and acted unprofessionally. (You don't invoke lawyers with the first invoice.) Instead of going with the flow and saying, "No problem, let me know when you're ready for the next stage," I had a snit and lost the client for good. Nothing I could ever do afterward restored their faith in me. They never gave me another assignment.

Exercise

Make a commitment to being courteous at all times in your professional dealings. This does not mean giving in, rolling over and playing dead when someone tries to exploit you. It simply means you can draw lines in the sand without losing your temper or raising your voice. If you're able to conduct a negotiation or navigate a difficulty with a client or editor without being impolite, you've just won yourself a supporter, even if, in the end, you don't agree to terms with the other person. For example, you may have an editor who wants you to make some changes to your manuscript. Instead of pulling a self-righteous "how dare you mess with my prose!" attitude, consider whether the suggested edits make sense and improve the work. Then courteously point out that while you agree that some reorganization is necessary, you disagree that all those commas need to be taken out. In most cases, if you have a reason for doing what you're doing, the editor will agree.

In the same way, if your check is late, you don't need to toss out an irate e-mail addressed to "the blood-sucking publisher in charge of this two-bit operation" but rather phrase your concern about payment as a gentle inquiry into the matter of when you might expect the check to be in the mail. Only after several attempts to get paid have failed should you resort to grievance officers, attorneys and the like. And even then you can resort to them without being discourteous.

Remember, being courteous is easy when everyone is being courteous to you. It's when the other party is being a jerk that your will to be courteous is tested. Understand that this is a test, and that your calm courtesy will often work to defuse a tense, even hostile situation. Also, you won't be taking on other people's problems and burdens as your own. They're responsible for their behavior; you're responsible for yours.

20
Integrity in all actions
creates confidence

Like courtesy, integrity is a character trait martial artists try to cultivate. For the martial artist, integrity means not letting your instructor, your school or yourself down by being dishonest. The martial artist represents her martial art at all times. If she acts in a way that reflects poorly on her, it also reflects poorly on the martial art, the instructor who trained her and the school where she trains. So the martial artist who lacks integrity hurts more than herself, she hurts many people around her.

Integrity isn't always rewarded, but the martial artist with integrity can be trusted by other people to act justly and fairly at all times. In training, integrity isn't just about not telling lies to people or not pretending you're a higher rank than you really are. Having integrity means working just as hard when no one's watching as when the judges' eyes are on you. It means committing to training even when you have competing demands on your time. It means not saying one thing to your friends in the school and another thing to the instructor. If others see you have integrity, they will have confidence in you and trust you—to teach them, to train with them, to befriend them.

For the writer, possessing integrity should be non-negotiable. In *remembered rapture: the writer at work*, author bell hooks says, "It takes critical vigilance not to be swept away by all the forces of materialist greed that encourage any writer eager to be more successful to dispense with integrity in the interest of making the big deals." She says, "Young writers . . . see the issues of ethics and integrity as concerns of the naive, of those who a young agent suggested to me are just not 'hungry enough.' When I came to New York I believed that it would be possible to garner greater financial reward for work well done, acquire a larger audience for my work, and maintain my integrity as a writer. Experience has confirmed that all this is possible."

Exercise

Don't fall into the common trap of promising more than you can deliver. Writers often agree to all sorts of things in order to win a writing project—and then promptly disappoint the client by being unable to fulfill the assignment. A common example is a tight deadline. A writer, eager to get the assignment, agrees to have the article finished by Monday (when it's Friday afternoon), but can't deliver when an essential interviewee proves to be out of town for the weekend. In this case, having integrity means not making guarantees you can't fulfill. It also means owning up to mistakes and poor judgment and accepting responsibility for the consequences. In fact, it's better to under-promise and over-deliver, as the business gurus like to say. Among other things, you come across as a person with integrity, one that your clients can count on.

The next time you're asked to take on a project that may be out of your league, may be difficult to do in the time allotted, or may be impossible to finish for the promised fee, take some time to consider how not performing adequately will reflect more poorly on you than turning down the assignment will. That doesn't mean you have to turn down the assignment. It just means you may have to renegotiate certain aspects of the deal. If you'll have lots of expenses writing a certain article, maybe the editor can cover your expenses. If the deadline is too tight, maybe it can be extended by a few days. Maybe you can involve a co-author as an expert. Instead of focusing on how much you want the job, focus on how you can do the job best, so the client is completely satisfied (and so that you are, too.)

21

The warrior does not reflect on past deeds while in battle

When a martial artist first begins sparring against real opponents or sparring partners, in general she focuses on one thing only—trying not to get hurt. At a slightly more advanced level, she focuses on trying not to look stupid. At some point in her training, when she becomes a warrior, she focuses on sparring to the best of her ability. To do this, she cannot worry about what she did yesterday when she sparred. Of course she must learn from her mistakes—and from her successes. If she leads with her head and she keeps getting kicked in the head, then obviously she must learn to keep her head guarded. But when she steps into the ring, what matters is how she spars in this match.

It doesn't matter if her sparring partner is of a superior rank with superior skills. She may not be able to win the match. But her effort and focus go toward sparring as well as she can. It doesn't matter if her sparring partner is a beginner with fewer skills. She cannot underestimate her opponent—a lucky kick could mean the less-experienced fighter wins. Instead, she concentrates on making the most of her own skills. It doesn't matter if she sparred with the same partner yesterday and won, or if she sparred with the same partner yesterday and lost. What matters is this match, and this match only. She cannot carry past deeds into battle with her.

For writers, this concept helps them continue to write in the face of obstacles and failures. It doesn't matter if yesterday all you wrote was gibberish. It doesn't matter if your last ten query letters were rejected, no matter how nasty the rejections were. (I was once told by an editor to get out of the writing business.)

What matters is that you focus on your writing today. Forget what happened yesterday. This doesn't mean that you try not to learn anything. It means you focus on doing the best you can right now, without obsessing about what has happened before. If you sit down at the computer and say to yourself, "Why do I bother? No one published my last book," you're focusing on the wrong thing. Writing a book that no one published contributed to your growth as a writer. No martial artist gets in the ring the first time and manages to do anything more than look frightened and back away. But with experience, she does better. She masters the techniques and the skills needed to be successful in the ring. With each writing project you do, you're also mastering the techniques and skills needed to be successful in the ring. So think of those past encounters as training for the future, and approach each new writing session with only one focus: to do the best you can for today.

When you sit down to write, dismiss the discouraging thoughts that might be running through your mind. (The power of affirmation is astonishing.) Replace any negative thoughts with positive ones. When you think, "Why should I send out ten more query letters when my last ten were rejected?" remind yourself that writers are persistent and that those last ten queries just didn't find the right target. Maybe one of the next ten will.

Think of yourself as that warrior going into battle. No one said it was going to be easy. No one ever promised you that you could head into battle and not risk getting wounded. But if you head into battle remembering how you got hurt the last five times, you're focusing on the wrong thing—and you're not going to fight very well. You'll be focused on not getting hurt instead of on winning. If all you're trying to do is not get hurt, why are you in the battle in the first place? Instead, go into battle knowing you're going to win this time, or die in the attempt. (Figuratively speaking.)

22

Know the vital points

A martial artist trains to attack the vulnerable spots of his opponent's anatomy. He doesn't kick the thigh, he kicks the knee or the groin. He doesn't punch the abdomen, he punches the ribs, the nose or the throat. The martial artist knows that an effective attack to a vital point—a vulnerable spot—will enable him to win the fight. Because he knows this, he is also careful to guard his own vital points so the opponent doesn't attack them.

In writing, whether fiction, nonfiction or poetry, you need to know the vital points. The vital points are those ideas and concepts that you're trying to communicate to your readers. In nonfiction, you might ask yourself, "What are the three things the readers should walk away from this article knowing?" and focus on providing those three things. In poetry, you need to know what emotion you're trying to evoke. In fiction, your main work is to create characters and plot that set up and resolve the conflict. The success of your short story or novel hinges on your ability to focus on these vital points.

E x e r c i s e

Evaluate where and how you can "know the vital points" in your writing to improve your work. Are you like many writers, and spend months researching instead of writing? If so, develop a basic outline of the information you must know, get that research done, then start writing, and fill in the blanks as you go along (this is how Mary Higgins Clark works). Do you send out hundreds of queries and generate little interest? Then focus on a specific magazine, figure out its audience, determine what type of articles are usually run (Service pieces or profiles? What style and tone? How many words?), then write a specific query to a specific editor on the masthead. Chances are good that this query (or another like it) will find its mark. In your fiction, make sure you understand that conflict is the vital point to your story or novel.

Identify the main conflict (in a romantic suspense novel, the conflict might be expressed as, "Will he kill her or kiss her?") and develop it and other less important conflicts to make your work memorable.

23

A strike is stronger than a push

Early in training, martial artists learn to strike—that is, to concentrate on hitting the target quickly and powerfully. If they move more slowly, they're not striking, they're pushing. And a push is not as effective as a strike, generally speaking. Think of slapping someone as opposed to just pressing your hand against them. One is forceful, stinging, and commands their attention; the other is merely irritating but of little consequence. (It's also easier to block and counter a push, whereas a slap or strike is over by the time the opponent can respond.)

Martial artists work to acquire speed and agility in order to deliver these stinging strikes that will disorient, disarm or disable an attacker.

In writing a story or an article, the ability to strike won't disorient, disarm or disable the reader (one hopes) but rather will grab his attention.

Writer Mary Shafer says, "People don't have the patience to read through a bunch of slow-moving background material before getting to the reward of becoming invested in the character(s) and their stories. Open with a

WHAM!—a moment of intense activity, involvement or consequence—and you've got them from the word 'go.'"

For your very next writing project, focus on composing a strike rather than a push. In your query letter, make the first sentence eye-popping. Give the editor a reason to read further. Choose the essential, telling details and arrange them in such a way that the editor has to read the entire letter and think about it before responding. In your novel, story or article, start out strong. Make the opening a strike. Grab the reader by the throat and shake him (metaphorically speaking, of course). Think of a quick strike that gets the reader's attention. Strip the information you include down to the necessary and essential and not an ounce more—in other words, no padding. This goes for fiction and nonfiction alike. Keep it lean, quick and powerful.

24
Mastery requires patience

When a martial artist begins training, she may make progress quickly—she learns how to perform a sidekick effectively, she learns a form (*kata*) early in her training— but eventually she comes to realize the difference between performing a technique *correctly,* and *mastering* the technique. Mastering the technique requires patience and perseverance. It requires repeating the technique thousands of times, as perfectly as possible. Many martial artists say that mastery is actually impossible, that there is always more to learn about a technique, and that there's always room for improvement.

In martial arts, experience is necessary for mastery. No matter how physically talented a person is, no matter how many sports she has played, she can't get around having to learn through experience. She learns that it's harder to do a form when judges are watching you at a promotion test than it is when they're not, that it's harder to spar less-skilled opponents than you'd think, that sometimes the board doesn't break even when you're sure you did the kick perfectly. But these experiences combine to make the martial artist into a true warrior.

Likewise, the writer may have some talent and tools to start with, but mastering the craft of writing takes experience and patience. Most writers who've made a success of their careers report that it was much harder and required much more time than they thought it would. Most writing careers develop slowly, over time—very few people achieve any kind of success early in their careers. It took me many years to understand everything a nonfiction author needs to understand about writing and promoting a book. The famous editor Sol Stein, in *Stein on Writing*, says, "By practice one learns to use what one has understood. Only writers, it seems, expect to achieve some level of mastery without practice." Ouch. Yet in my coaching I am often approached by writers who want to know, "How can I get a six-figure advance for my first novel like so-and-so?" when the question they should be asking is, "How can I become the best writer I can be?" I was once surprised, depressed and repelled all at the same time when a writing magazine had an article in which the writer said, "You don't even have to be a good writer to break into this field!" As if that were somehow a good thing. As a writer, mastery should be your goal. And mastery takes patience.

Exercise

Be willing to do what it takes. Only those who devote extensive time and energy to developing the craft will be rewarded by it. If you start now (instead of next year when you'll have more time), you'll inevitably move closer each day to the goals you dream of achieving as a writer. Choose to master the craft by writing every day and by learning every day. Keep a writing journal that follows your progress as you struggle to achieve your writing dreams, and record the successes and near misses that you encounter.

25

Cultivate perfect awareness

The martial artist learns to always be aware of his environment. If he's walking down the street on the way to the corner convenience store for a quart of milk, he's aware of what's going on around him, if other people are on the street, what the terrain is like, what the weather is doing. If he's in conversation with someone else, he's aware of what's happening around him while still paying attention to his companion. If he has had an experience that preoccupies his mind, he doesn't just stumble home or follow his automatic route and arrive, not remembering the drive.

He keeps his perception functioning and on alert at all times.

Not only does this help him anticipate an attack, but it helps him avoid routine problems, upsets and frustrations that annoy other people. When he notices the cars on the road ahead of him slowing down, he pays attention to determine what's happening and maybe takes an alternate route home instead of passing all the slow-moving drivers only to find himself stuck in the middle of a traffic jam. He perceives changes in the people around him so that he can have that talk with his wife before she walks out on him. Cultivating perfect awareness helps the warrior overcome challenges in his life.

For the writer, being aware, cultivating awareness, results in better writing. A person who is aware of the cadences of a certain dialect creates a more realistic story. A writer who knows what the weather feels like just before the tornado hits gains the confidence of her readers. A writer who can describe the clothes that teenagers wear helps her readers enter into the world of teenagers. A writer who relies on the experiences of others (she read about it in a book) does not seem as compelling to us.

Awareness helps writers come up with stories and articles. Understanding the trends by listening to what her friends are talking about and paying attention to what challenges and problems are upsetting a community helps a writer deliver what editors need. Letting the environment stimulate ideas helps the writer stay fresh and interested in conveying her stories.

Exercise

Practice your observation skills. Make it a game. Walk into your living room, glance around for fifteen or thirty seconds, then shut your eyes and ask yourself what color the carpet is, what position the drapes are in, what objects are in the room that don't belong there, what activities, if any, are taking place.

Try this game whenever you leave the house: As you lock the door behind you, sweep the neighborhood with a glance, then close your eyes or turn your back (umm . . . maybe not if you live in a really bad neighborhood), and name which neighbors are out cutting their grass, what the sky looks like, and whose garage door is open. (Or whichever details are relevant.) As you progress in skill, you'll see your writing takes on a richer character, and you become a more solid storyteller.

26

Do not fear the blow

Beginning martial artists often have an exaggerated fear of getting hit. (In some cases, it was this very fear that brought them to martial arts in the first place.) When they spar, all they can think is how much it would hurt if their opponent hit them. This fear makes them awkward and it clouds their thoughts. It's hard to protect yourself *and* counterattack at the same time, and if all you can think is how much that punch is going to hurt, it's hard to think instead about how to avoid or counter it. Someone who fears the blow always stays on the defensive and tries to cover up. This is not the way to win a fight or a battle. (Although sometimes duck-and-cover has its place.)

After some experience—the martial artist has been kicked and punched and thrown a few times—he learns that he always gets up again. In other words, the blow doesn't hurt as much as he expected; or if it did hurt as much as he expected, it didn't render him incapable of responding or protecting himself. It was just a blow. It doesn't have to totally disorient and destroy him. From then on, he can do what needs to be done without being afraid of what will happen to him. He knows he risks getting hit, but it doesn't obsess him or prevent him from taking action.

For the writer, the same process must occur. The first rejection is painful (so you might as well get it over with). If you fear the blow, you'll never have a chance to succeed.

Veteran writer Linda Formichelli says, "I recently tallied up all the responses I'd gotten to queries in the last six years and found that 62 percent of my ideas had been rejected. If I feared the blow, I would have quit years ago—because that's a lot of blows to the ego." Instead, Linda enjoys a prosperous career of writing for magazines (and penning the occasional book).

E x e r c i s e

Treat rejection letters merely as the information that this particular editor is not interested in pursuing this particular idea at this time. That's it. It's no comment on your abilities, skills or potential as a writer, even if the editor is nasty enough to so imply.

The best way to "not fear the blow" of rejection is to have a thorough plan for each piece you're working on before you send it out. I might, for example, send a query letter out to ten editors I think will be interested in an article I want to write. I will also create a list of thirty more editors to send the query to if the first ten pass on it. If all forty editors reject the idea, then I'll revisit it and perhaps re-envision it, then send it out again. Or, I will set it aside but keep it on my project list to return to later when something has changed in my career or the marketplace to make the idea more appealing. (I had the idea for the book that became *Dojo Wisdom* years ago, but I envisioned it in an entirely different format. I had to find my current agent to finally sell the book.)

Create a plan of action and you'll know what to do so you won't have to fear the blow.

27

Your beliefs guide your strategy

Martial artists agree that martial arts techniques should never be used to attack another person, only to defend oneself or another person who is under attack. Many martial arts masters believe that if you actually get into a fight with another person, you've failed, at some level, as a martial artist. The training a martial artist receives is intended to prevent violence, not provoke it. A martial artist, working from this belief, creates a strategy based on the principle of nonviolence. In other words, he plans how not to fight. In any burgeoning conflict, he will walk away if he can. He will use different techniques to de-escalate the situation. He will call in the authorities. He will apologize even if he's not in the wrong if he thinks it will calm the situation. He will say, and mean, "I don't want to fight." In other words, instead of paying lipservice to his belief in nonviolence and then happily wading in with fists swinging, he will make certain his actions always coincide with his beliefs.

A writer's beliefs should also guide his strategy. When I first began writing, I was able to get a couple of books about martial arts published. I also had a few other books on different subjects published. I didn't want to be known as "just" a writer who specialized in martial arts, but those projects kept coming my way, so I wrote them. Finally, I realized that I was doing important work. Martial arts had saved my life. I had found it tremendously empowering. Why wouldn't I want to bring the power to other people? Once I realized that I believed strongly and wholeheartedly in my message, and stopped selling it short, I created a strategy for bringing my ideas to people who weren't martial artists. This strategy increased my success as a writer, bringing me more into the mainstream (where I had originally wanted to go).

I often read books on how to make money as a writer and if you believe these books, it seems the only people who make money are business writers—people who produce ad copy, brochures and the like. This is certainly work that needs to be done, and if it's work that you want to do and enjoy doing, more power to you. But I've tried it and dislike it intensely. I don't believe it's a legitimate use of my time and energy. Forcing myself to spend my creative energy on writing I don't believe in would be a foolish waste—and poor strategy. I'd rather have a day job at an insurance company and write books in my spare time, if I

had to make the choice. However, I make a fine living doing the kind of writing I believe in. You can, too—if you
create a conscious strategy that coincides with your beliefs.

Exercise

What are your core beliefs? What message do you want to bring
to the world as a writer? What kind of writing appeals to you?
What do you think you could be successful doing? Answering
these questions can help you devise the right strategy for achieving writing success. Don't suppose that just because it's harder to
make a living writing novels than nonfiction that you shouldn't
bother trying to write fiction. If it's that important to you, then
create a strategy for writing—and selling—your novels. A person
who wants to write for magazines for a living will pursue a very
different strategy from someone who wants to work as a writing
consultant for businesses. Determine your beliefs—what's important to you—then let your strategy flow from that.

28
Self-consciousness prevents action

The bad guys count on our desire not to make a scene in
order to take advantage of us. They don't want to draw attention to themselves, and they don't want you to draw attention to them, either. They want to grab your purse or
shove you into the waiting car with a minimum of fuss.

Martial artists know that making a scene is an extremely effective deterrent and a highly useful self-defense

technique. In fact, one Department of Justice study found that 50 percent of physical assaults could be prevented or stopped if the defender shouted. That's right, if the defender, the person being attacked, just shouted, half the time the attacker would go away. That's a pretty powerful tool. So why isn't it used more? Because people are self-conscious. They freeze, afraid to act because they might embarrass themselves. Because they're not positive they're reading the danger signals right and they don't want to embarrass the poor guy who was just walking to his car. They don't want people to hear them scream and then make fun of them for overreacting.

But the fact is, self-consciousness prevents effective action. If you did scream, and the attacker wasn't really an attacker, is that such a big deal? Is it worth the risk of not screaming? Martial artists know it's more sensible to act now and not worry if it's a little embarrassing later.

For writers, self-consciousness creates an enormous stumbling block to success. Writer Ruth Gruen, a PR expert and former book editor, says, "There is, in most writers, a little voice that sits on our shoulder and tells us we are a) ridiculous; b) no good; c) wasting our time and d) who do we think we are that anyone would want to read what we have to say anyway?" That pretty much sums up the situation for the majority of writers starting out. Ruth says, "Ignore it. Let it blather on but understand it is the voice of your own insecurity and negativity and it doesn't know what it's talking about. If you work consistently, ethically and patiently, you will write what is the best you can do. And that will almost always be wonderful." As for that little voice? "It goes away," Ruth says. "Trust me."

Writer Linda Formichelli puts the concept of forgetting self-consciousness in practical terms. "I have no shame. I toot my own horn (loudly) in my queries, I call editors, I ask strangers for assignments. If you're afraid of what others will think of you, it can keep you from getting your work out there. I know my writing is good, I know my ideas are solid, and if one editor doesn't agree, there are others who will."

Exercise

Create a series of affirmations to use whenever doubts and self-consciousness threaten to get in the way of being a productive writer who puts her work out there. You can keep them in a journal you read each day or post them on the wall above your computer. An affirmation can be any positive statement that makes you feel good about what you do. It may be something your mother said to you, or a quotation from a writer you admire. It may be something good a teacher said about writing, or a nice review of your book, or anything personally meaningful and inspiring. But it's always positive, and it's something that makes you feel confident when you see it and when you say it.

As an example, I once took a position that was unpopular in certain parts of the martial arts world. I received some negative feedback from people. A friend, knowing I was in the middle of a controversy and wishing I'd stuck with teaching for a living, sent me a quotation: "You can tell the warrior by the arrows in her forehead." It was so appropriate that I had it hanging on my wall for years. Every time I lost heart or received criticism, I looked at that saying, remembered the kindness and support of my friend, and kept on writing.

29

Aiki, the impassive mind, brings strength

Very early in their training, martial artists learn that fear, doubt and confusion make it difficult for them to function effectively. If they're afraid of getting hit or of hitting another person, they don't act with confidence and power. If they're in doubt as to what they should do next, their very hesitation can be used against them. If they're confused about the best way to respond to an attack, they'll be limited in how quickly they can respond.

So a martial artist learns to empty her mind of fear and self-doubt, of anger and indecision. She strives for a state of detachment, called *aiki,* or the impassive mind. She may care deeply about what's happening, but she sets that emotion aside until she has acted effectively.

A writer who develops *aiki* is much stronger in her decision-making than one who doesn't. For writers, it's crucial. Otherwise, it's easy to be exploited (and many scoundrels rely on writers to make ill-considered decisions). For example, suppose you've sent a manuscript to an agent and she says, "I love your manuscript! I'd like to represent it, and I'll need $2,000 up front." Because you're thrilled at the prospect of being represented by an agent, you may be inclined to scrape together the $2,000 and send it to the agent, hoping for miracles.

However, if you set aside the excitement you feel and instead seek to make the decision logically and rationally, you'd do a little research and find that legitimate agents don't charge fees upfront—they make their money from selling your work. So far from being an excellent opportunity for you, this would just be a waste of two thousand hard-earned dollars.

Suppose you're talking to a magazine editor about a potential project, and he outlines the work he needs done, and says, "We can pay $500. Can you have it done by next week?" The pressure to make a decision quickly could force you to say yes to both the fee and the deadline. Yet maybe the fee won't reimburse you for your time (and experience). And maybe the deadline means you'll have to work through your son's birthday. If you cultivate *aiki,* instead of feeling pressured and worried about losing the opportunity if you don't agree immediately, you'll say, "Let me calculate the work involved in doing a good job for you. May I call you back with my answer later this afternoon?" You have a lot more to lose if you make a decision under pressure without considering all of the facts.

Exercise

High-pressure sales—you must act now or lose the chance forever—are designed to force you to act impulsively, without thinking through all the consequences. You can be sure you'll regret saying yes, but you'll never regret saying no. (In fact, I have serenely turned down any number of "once in a lifetime opportunities" without actually spoiling my lifetime.) To put the brakes on making impulsive, poorly thought-out and regrettable professional decisions, remember that the pressure to make this professional decision is just as artificial as the pressure involved in the hard sell. Just as you recognize the hard sell when the telemarketer calls, you can recognize the hard sell in your professional life—the temptation to make a hasty decision based on not enough information simply because someone is pressuring you. The next time you feel confused, elated, distracted or distraught and feel forced to make a decision in that mental state, simply say, "No." Tell the other party, "I need to think about this," or "I don't have time right now, but I'll get back with you later in the week." Rarely is any professional decision so urgent that taking the opportunity to think about it means losing it, and it's usually better to risk losing the opportunity than to commit yourself to a project, an agent, an editor or a financial commitment that's not right for you.

30

Persist even when you are fatigued

A martial artist (and in fact any athlete) improves her performance and endurance by training even when she's tired and wants to stop. Partway through the training session, she may want to go sit down and take a breather. But she doesn't, because persisting even when she's fatigued actually builds her endurance and her reserves of strength. If she doesn't quit this time, next time she can go longer without feeling fatigued. Trying to perform the techniques perfectly even when her legs feel like spaghetti teaches her to reach into and cultivate her inner reserves of strength—reserves she might not have realized existed.

A fighter must have the ability to continue even when fatigued. Often, the person who wins the match or the fight isn't the one with the knock-out punch. It's the one who's still standing in the tenth round—the one with the stamina, endurance and grit to keep going even when flat-out exhausted and completely drained.

This plays into the writing life in a couple of ways. First, many writers face actual physical and mental fatigue, especially if you have a day job and a family that needs your attention. Second, after weeks, months and even years of getting piles of rejection letters, you have an excuse to plead exhaustion with the whole business and give up.

But instead of using "I'm too tired" as an excuse not to write and not to send your work out into the world, the warrior-writer does it anyway.

Exercise

Practice writing even when you feel tired and drained. Remember that often the difference between a published, successful author and one who's not is that the published, successful author went ahead and wrote even if she didn't particularly feel like it—and so got the writing done instead of finding excuses for not doing it.

Your writing-while-tired piece can simply be a journal entry, or it can be an actual article or a scene from a novel or a short story you're trying to complete for publication. It doesn't matter as long as you discipline yourself to write even though you may not feel like it. An unexpected bonus I have found is that if I tackle a complicated or less desirable task when I'm tired, I censor myself less, write more naturally and accessibly and just do the task and get it done without a lot of hand-wringing over it.

31

One who is humble can never be overcome

Imagine the martial arts master who struts into a room full of black belts from various disciplines and says, "You're a pathetic group of martial artists! I can beat every single one of you without even breaking a sweat!" Arrogant? Yes. About to be stomped into the ground? Yep. Contrast this with the martial arts master who walks into that same room and says, "If you'd like, I'll show you some techniques that have worked for me." Humble? Yes. About to be stomped into the ground? Of course not. The black belts in the room have nothing to prove to the martial arts master. They have no need to stomp him into the ground. They're likely to believe he has something useful to show them because he's not putting them down and insulting them. If they don't want what he has to offer, that's a matter of indifference to him. He is humble. He doesn't need universal approval and adoring students prostrating themselves at his feet to feed his ego.

The martial artist who doesn't have to puff himself up but is humble about his abilities and skills rarely finds himself forced to use those abilities and skills to defend himself. When he is forced to fight, it's because he has no other choice, and therefore he is mentally, emotionally, and physically prepared to defeat the opponent no matter what happens. He is utterly committed to winning the fight. He has exhausted all other possibilities. Imagine trying to overcome *that* warrior. Not going to be very easy to do, no matter how good you are.

This doesn't mean that, as a writer, you have to keep quiet and humble about your skills and abilities. In fact, that's likely to backfire (remember *Lesson #28: Self-consciousness prevents action.*) But it does mean that you should be humble enough to believe that you don't know everything. The writer who is open to new ideas and new ways of doing things will become a better writer. The best-selling mystery author Lawrence Block wrote in his column for *Writers' Digest,* "It's easy for me to run short of humility. . . . It takes arrogance, doesn't it, to sit down at a typewriter making up stories out of the whole cloth and expecting total strangers to be caught up in them. . . . Humility helps me keep myself in perspective. When my humility is in good order, both success and failure become easier to take. . . . All I ever have to do is the best I can."

Being humble also means that instead of crowing about how brilliant and professional you are, you *show* your clients how brilliant and professional you are by turning in the copy they need on deadline, following their guidelines, and delivering the project within the price that you quoted.

Exercise

Avoid prima donna disorder (PDD). Writers, including me, occasionally find themselves having tantrums when some lesser editorial type dares to mess with their brilliant prose. PDD can strike any writer at any time, should be recognized immediately, and dealt with firmly and professionally.

Instead of responding to the first flash of resentment you

might feel when someone suggests, "This doesn't flow as smoothly as it could," control the impulse and instead of saying, "What would you know, you're illiterate!" say, "What would you suggest I do?" or "Can you clarify what exactly strikes you as un-developed about my characters?" Be open to learning about writing from others. And then be confident enough to disregard their suggestions when you know you're right. In other words, a humble writer can never be overcome.

Push beyond your limits

A martial artist trains to go beyond her perceived limits. When she has to learn the thirty-seven movements of *toi-gye* form and doubts she'll ever be able to do it, she tries anyway. By training to push beyond her limits, she extends her limits so that she can continually do more. If she never pushed her limits, she would confine herself to a small skill set of techniques, and she would not be able to trust that she could consistently do what needed to be done. A martial artist who constantly pushes her limits knows that she can do what she has to do.

For a writer, pushing beyond your limits means getting outside your comfort zone, doing work that's different from what you ordinarily do, creating work that's deeper than you tend to create. It may mean trying a different kind of writing you've never felt comfortable with. Maybe you don't feel you write good poetry, for example, so you stopped trying ten years ago. But if you don't push your limits, you won't gain much. Maybe you can learn to be a better poet. What is more likely is that the experience will give you a greater appreciation for using just the right word in just the right place, making all of your writing more accomplished. Author Bob Spear says, "When you go beyond your current abilities and boundaries, that's when you develop the most."

He's right. For years, I focused on book writing and told anyone who asked that I didn't write very many articles because I had trouble with them. I tried to write an article as if it were a very small book, which wasn't the right approach. But when the first book in this series, *Dojo Wisdom: 100 Simple Ways to Become a Stronger, Calmer, More Courageous Person,* was published, I wanted to promote the book. One of the ways I knew I could do this was by writing articles based on it for consumer magazines. I wasn't sure I could do it, but I pushed beyond my limits. I queried magazine editors. A patient editor at *American Fitness* helped me work out a nice piece on getting started in martial arts. An editor at *New Living* liked an article based on a concept presented in the book. Then an editor at *Family Circle* suggested that instead of an article about martial arts empowering women, I might try to write an essay about how martial arts empowered me. I did it, she bought the essay right away, and I ended up with an impressive publishing credit under my belt. Not only did this experience help me learn my craft better, but I also earned several thousand dollars.

Exercise

Choose a mode of writing you haven't done in quite some time because you think you're no good at it. Remember that this is your perception, and your perception can change. So can your skills. Maybe it's poetry or short stories or article writing or even writing an advertisement. Set aside some time on a regular basis (a few hours a week) to push your limits by working on that type of writing. You'll be amazed at how flexing your writing muscles in this way will improve your other writing projects. It will also give you the confidence to tackle projects that come your way even if you haven't done them before. ("A video script for show-casing your manufacturing business? No problem!" "A series of greeting cards for the believers-in-UFOs market? Got it!") Consciously choose to push your limits.

33

Master the present

A martial artist learns that he can't concern himself with the future to the exclusion of the present. Only by being here in the present can the martial artist be fully effective. Although the martial artist may plan and train for threats and challenges that haven't happened yet (but may happen in the future), he must always be aware of what is happening at the moment. If he's walking down the street, he's not focused on the task he'll be performing when he gets to the end of the street. He's focused on what's happening now—who else is walking down the street, what the weather is like, if he's just about to trip over that pothole. Just as the warrior does not reflect on past deeds while in battle *(Lesson #21),* he does not concentrate on the future and forget about the present.

Martial artists are realists. They understand that the warrior may not be here tomorrow, but if he focuses on today, he improves his chances of sticking around.

A writer must also be present for the journey, not just focused on the destination (the published book, the bestseller list, the take-this-job-and-shove-it speech you have all ready for your boss.) While it's good to look ahead occasionally—for example, the visualization exercise described in *Lesson #5: Meditate,* is about imagining the future—you need to remember the here and now.

Exercise

All too often, writers use the excuse that they're too busy now to actually sit down and write. They promise themselves that after they finish this huge project at work, they'll tackle that novel. They say that after the rush and fuss of Christmas ends, they'll take care of business. Or after their father recovers from being ill or once their children start school. Understand these excuses for what they are: excuses. The next time you hear yourself making an excuse, stop. Focus instead on what you can do in the present to further your writing goals. If you can only squeeze in ten minutes of writing time during your lunch hour, then do it. Give up today's television show in order to do today's writing. Go without makeup and use the extra ten minutes you gain for writing. Keep yourself firmly situated in what you can do right now to further your writing.

34

Understand the nature of yin-yang

Most martial arts, rooted in traditional Taoist beliefs about the nature of the universe, incorporate the concept of yin-yang. Simply put, yin-yang is the idea that the universe is made up of conflicting yet harmonious elements that work together to make a whole. Yin energy is passive; yang energy is active. These elements are complementary—one cannot exist without the other. What is light without dark? Hard without soft?

The goal is to find a balance between the opposite elements. It's not that light is better than dark or day should be accepted and night banned. It's not that one should never rest or that one should always rest. The ideal is that rest must be balanced with activity. This middle way of balance is the path that martial artists strive to take.

Understanding the nature of yin-yang helps a writer recognize that nothing is all good or all bad all of the time. When writing is going well and the writer is in the flow, it's likely that some challenge will come along to disrupt the flow, and the writer should remain as calm and accepting of the challenge as possible. In the same way, if you can remember yin-yang when you get the tenth rejection letter in a row, you'll understand that this negative will be balanced by something positive in your writing—perhaps a good writing session, or an opportunity you weren't expecting, or a phone call accepting an article you've been trying to place. In other words, just as we don't expect good news will last forever, we shouldn't expect that bad news will, either.

By creating balance in your writing life, you'll ultimately become more successful as a writer.

Exercise

Create balance in your writing life. The idea of balance is anathema to many writers. We tend to work like manic-depressives, as if we all had bipolar disorder. You know what I mean—you feel compelled into a fury of hard work, not even sleeping for three days, followed by a period of—I don't like to call it rest because it's more like deep despair. Once you climb out of the slough, you do it all over again. This out-of-balance routine is certainly not conducive to mental health, but it's very common for creative types to succumb. After all, when you feel energized, shouldn't you take advantage of that energy?

Of course, you should, but within certain limits. You can actually maintain that feeling of being energized over the long haul if you don't abuse yourself in the process. Instead of blindly following what appears to be the muse but which is really a ticket to the madhouse, insert some logic and reason into the writing process. Instead of writing only when you feel inspired—and then locking yourself in your room for three days without food or drink, writing furiously before the muse abandons you—write on a regular basis. Pursue balance. Make certain that you eat well and sleep well. If you put your pen down (or shut down the computer) even when you still feel you have something to say, you'll be that much more eager to approach your writing session the next day. And you'll be living a slightly saner, more balanced life.

35

Take small risks to build courage for large risks

When a martial artist first learns to spar, she isn't thrown into the ring and told to defend herself against a highly skilled black belt. Few people would do well against such an assault and it certainly wouldn't teach the beginner very many useful lessons, except maybe never to trust the instructor again. When a martial artist first begins training, she is given the tools that she will someday use in the sparring ring. She learns to block, to kick, to punch, to throw. She does these techniques to the air at first (no one gets hurt this way), then in highly controlled no contact or light contact drills. Then she begins using more power against padded targets or a heavy bag. Finally, she begins to spar against live opponents, but still under controlled conditions. As the martial artist becomes more comfortable, more contact is gradually allowed.

This slow buildup exposes the martial artist to small risks at first. By taking the small risks, she builds the courage to take larger risks. Taking risks requires tools, experience, savvy and confidence. These aren't usually acquired in one fell swoop. They must be acquired over time, as the martial artist learns to trust herself and as she develops the skills she needs to survive.

The same idea can be applied to the writing life. If you jump in with both feet and take a tremendous risk (quitting your day job without ever having sold a piece of writing, for example), you may not be prepared for what will happen, you may fail, and the experience may ultimately make you decide to quit pursuing your writing dreams.

A beginner just learning the craft and just discovering what it means to be a professional can take on small jobs and small challenges to build her confidence and succeed on a larger scale.

If you can handle writing a small project for a client, turning in good clean copy on deadline, not only will you feel more confident in your abilities, but the client will be more willing to hire you again, and to hire you for more significant work.

If you're longing to be published by *The New Yorker,* it makes good sense to hone your essay writing by starting with a local op-ed piece. I built my confidence in my essay writing bit by bit this way. I started with writing essays for newsletters for organizations I belonged to. I submitted an essay or two to a writers' contest and was encouraged when I placed high. Finally I sent an essay to *Family Circle,* which promptly accepted the piece. If I had tried to break into a high profile consumer magazine like that without taking smaller risks at first, I probably wouldn't have been successful. And, practically speaking, having clips (past publishing credits) didn't hurt when I approached *Family Circle.*

Exercise

If you're hesitant about putting your writing out in the world, start small. These small successes will help fuel your larger ones. Begin with a letter to the editor. Or supply an item for a newsletter for an organization you belong to (newsletter editors are almost always frantic for articles to fill their pages). Once you've had small successes like this, move on to the bigger challenges (too many writers stay small for too long). Take the bigger risk. Submit your article idea to a regional or national magazine. Agree to a project you've never tried before in order to challenge yourself and flex your writing muscles. Build your confidence through a series of steps of increasing risk and exposure and you'll make your writing dreams come true.

You cannot fail if you keep trying

The first time a martial artist walks into the *dojo* or the *dojang* (training hall) and performs a front kick, she doesn't do it perfectly, or even correctly. Does that mean she's a failure? Of course not. It just means she needs more practice. No one thinks she's a failure because she couldn't do the technique perfectly on the first try. Everyone understands that the first try is just the first step—important, even crucial, but still just the first step.

One of the important lessons in martial arts is that you can't fail if you keep trying. Imagine that you're in a self-defense situation. Your first kick hits the intended target, but it doesn't make the attacker let go. Do you give up and let the attacker do what he will? No. You keep trying. You do a second technique, and a third. You fight for all you're worth. Only if you give up have you failed to protect yourself.

Those martial artists who *give up* are failures. They

don't achieve black belt. Those who do achieve black belt didn't achieve it because the road was so smooth and free of challenges. They achieved the rank because, despite problems and pulled hamstrings, they kept trying.

After so many rejection letters it can be hard for a writer not to feel like a failure, and then give up. But remember that failing only happens *if* you give up, not before. So you can feel like a failure if you want, but you won't actually *be* a failure unless you stop trying.

In *Lesson #24*, I talked about how patience leads to mastery of craft. In the same way, patience and persistence lead to a rewarding career. Writer Linda Formichelli says, "I had been trying to break into the high-profile women's magazines, which pay one to two dollars per word, for two years. I sent query after query, and got rejection after rejection. But I didn't give up, and one day, an editor at *Woman's Day* called me up (possibly because she was sick of my good-but-not-quite-right queries) and gave me a couple of tips for querying her magazine." Linda followed her advice and sold her next idea for close to $3,000. "If I hadn't persevered through dozens of rejections," she says, "I'd still be writing for mags that pay 20 cents per word." Because she never gave up, Linda made her dream of writing for high-profile women's magazines a reality—now a routine reality.

The first book Alice Sebold, author of the best-selling novel *The Lovely Bones,* published was a modestly successful memoir. As she says, "Nothing else mattered to me as much as great books and wanting to try to write." She couldn't find a publisher for her first two novels, but she kept persisting. Eventually she achieved enormous writing success.

Exercise

All happily published writers have stories about persevering through rejection and having to believe in themselves when no one else would. That's the nature of the writing life. The ability to keep trying even after rejection is what separates the ultimately successful writers from the unsuccessful ones. It's not great talent or connections, but simple bullheadedness that makes the difference.

The next time a rejection letter, negative criticism, or unpleasant critique makes you feel like hanging up your pen, remind yourself that this is just the first step on the road. With each rejection letter, you learn more about the business and about the craft. Eventually you will succeed. Put it this way: Are you going to let this person (this overworked editorial assistant, this picky English teacher, this nasty literary agent) prevent you from achieving your dreams by convincing you to give up? Of course not. You won't let them talk you into failing. You'll continue despite what they say and do.

37

Act on your intention

When the martial artist sees an opening, he immediately acts, striking to the target. His actions flow directly from his intentions: he sees the target, he intends to strike the target, and he strikes to the target. He does not put a lot of thought and decision-making into this effort. He doesn't question himself, "Is this the best opening I'll see? Should I really commit myself to the strike?" He simply does what he has trained to do. If he doesn't act directly from intention but hesitates, the opening disappears and he may lose the match.

The martial artist intends to be the best warrior he can be, so he trains often and consistently. Again, his actions flow from his intentions. He doesn't think about all the other things he'd rather be doing. He intends to be the best warrior he can be, so he trains the way a warrior should.

Writers often set their intentions but forget that they need to have a plan for following through. Consider how every January people decide all the things they're going to do differently this year, but by February these resolutions have fallen by the wayside, which is littered with all sorts of good intentions.

In other words, you have to act on your intention. If you want to get published this year, you have to do more than write that down as a goal. You have to break it into steps that you can follow to make your dream become a reality.

E x e r c i s e

Writer, consultant and coach Bev Bachel advises writers to make a list of the most important goals they have. Writers should have a mix of long-term and short-term goals, the short-term goals being steps needed to reach the long-term goals, she says. The goals should be measurable and specific. Instead of making "become a freelance writer" a goal, try, "earn $40,000 from freelance writing projects this year." The second is specific and measurable. You'll know if you've gotten there. It also gives you an idea of what your short-term goals should be. For example, you'll need to decide where that $40,000 is going to come from. Magazine article sales? Corporate communications? The answer will depend on your abilities and interests and the background and contacts you already have in place.

Once you've made a list of your long-term goals, consider what your goals for this year will be. Then make a list of what needs to be accomplished each month, and then each week, in order to meet those goals. Forcing yourself to work through the steps and see the amount of work involved helps you become successful, Bev says. You know what you're in for, and you're not surprised or upset when it ends up taking a lot of work to make your dreams a reality.

Bev also encourages writers to find a "goal buddy." This is a person with whom you can share your short- and long-term goals, and to whom you report in on a regular basis, to help keep you on track. The relationship is reciprocal—you help your buddy stay focused on goals, too. People with a goal buddy tend to stick with their goals and make more progress, Bev says.

38

Focus on the Way

Martial artists know they've started on a journey. While the destination—be it mastery, a black belt, or some other goal—entices them, it's not the most important consideration. If the martial artist focuses only on getting his black belt, without also enjoying the journey of learning new skills and appreciating what his body can do, he is missing the point.

The Buddhist monk Thich Nhat Hanh once said, "The destination of life is death. But if we focus on death, we can't enjoy life." Instead of focusing on death, focus on life. Instead of focusing on the end result, focus on the journey. Martial artists learn this lesson in their training.

As I described in *Lesson #37, Act on your intention*, focusing on your goals is important. You may want to be published, so you take steps to achieve that goal. If you didn't have the goal, you wouldn't be able to reach it. But now and then you should also realize that the destination isn't the only point, that the journey matters, too. You can still be a fulfilled writer just because you're writing, whether you ever get published or not. If you focus only on getting published, you miss the journey. You miss the beauty and delight of writing something that astonishes and touches others.

Once I started having financial success as a writer, I began to focus on making a living and providing a good life for my daughter. I tended to think of every writing project in this way: How much money will I make? Will this contribute to my ability to buy a house for Jessica and me? These are not bad or wrong questions. They need to be asked if you're hoping to survive and thrive as a professional writer. But they were the *only* questions I was asking. I was focused only on results. I had lost sight of the journey.

During this period, I began writing a memoir about my experiences with my daughter, who is severely disabled. Having some difficulty with it, I consulted with Tom

Lorenz, a writing teacher I'd had at the university. I sat in his small office, and told him I was having trouble with the memoir. I was concerned because I was spending a lot of time on it and I wasn't sure if anyone would publish it.

Tom looked at me as if I had lost my mind. "Umm," he said. "Is that the most important thing? What about just writing it because it needs to be written?"

I sat there, stunned. Of course. Why not write the book just because it needed to be written? Just because I had to, without worrying about who would publish it and how big of an advance I would get. So I did it, I wrote the memoir. It still hasn't sold to a publisher, but that's completely beside the point. It was an exhausting, painful journey, but one I'm grateful I embarked on. It helped me heal and accept a different life from the one I expected. Now and then I reflect on passages I've written in the memoir, and it helps me cope. It helps me see how far I've come. I'd say writing the memoir was worth every minute, even if I never see a dime from it. The destination doesn't matter. Writing the memoir was the journey.

E x e r c i s e

If you've lost the fire and passion you once had for writing, it's probably because you've become focused on the results (destination) instead of the journey. While writers do need to keep their eye on whether the check for the article has come in or not, it shouldn't be the main focus of their days. If writing has become a grind, you've probably stopped thinking of it as a journey of exploration. That doesn't mean you'll never feel passion about your writing again. It just means you have to give yourself permission to write something that will never see the light of day, that will never be published, that will never add a cent to your coffers. Set aside some time to write pieces that will never get you closer to your writing goals. I give myself an hour a day to work on a novel. I don't care if the novel never gets published. I love working on it. It makes me feel energized. It gives me a different kind of writing to grapple with than the usual run of nonfiction I do during the day. Give yourself permission to enjoy the journey without worrying about the final destination.

39
Chi overcomes obstacles

Martial artists use Chi, or life energy, to perform difficult tasks, as I discussed in *Lesson #4: From your Chi flows your creativity*. The shout you hear martial artists use—the *kihop* or *kiai*—is the physical expression of this energy. The martial artist trying to break a concrete block will summon his Chi and release it (through the shout) at the moment of impact. By focusing all his energy, will and force on the task, the martial artist succeeds.

When martial artists train, they know if they keep going even when they're tired, they'll build up reserves of Chi that they can call upon when needed. They're convinced that this inner energy will help them overcome all obstacles.

For writers, creating and drawing on that inner energy also helps them overcome obstacles. To summon your Chi, you need to clear your mind from distractions and worries and instead focus simply on tapping into the creative energy you have inside. Silence the inner critic who harps on all your failings. Disregard the pleas of the boss who needs you to work late "just this once" for the fifth time in a row. Use meditation techniques to clear your mind and focus on your goal, which is to write well, without difficulty and blocks. Visualize a successful writing session, one in which you feel very good about what you've done afterward.

Exercise

Breathing techniques can help you find your Chi and use it. Korean martial artists use breathing and stretching techniques from the healing art of Impo, which is something like Chi Kung and T'ai Chi. Use this sequence to renew and tap into your Chi.

Begin with a very simple series of controlled breaths. Close your eyes and breathe deeply in through your nose, then out through your mouth. As you repeat this breathing, take a longer period of time to inhale and a correspondingly longer time to exhale. Deliberately feel your shoulders and neck relax as you breathe.

Once you feel as if some of the burden of the day has dropped from your shoulders, move to a series of cleansing breaths. Stand while doing these to feel the Chi moving through your body. Keep your feet comfortably apart, arms relaxed. Inhale through the nose and gently extend your arms out to the side to expand your chest cavity and give your lungs room to take in all the air they can. Now, breathe out through your mouth—but not the typical way. Instead, use "fogging breath." Think about how you breathe on your glasses to fog them up so you can clean them, or the way you breathe to fog up the window on a winter's day. This fogging breath cleanses your body of toxins and helps stir your Chi. As you exhale, bring your arms together in front of you, as if you were pushing your hands together in order to get rid of all the air in your lungs. (If you start to yawn while doing this exercise, that's okay, just keep persisting.) Repeat this breathing technique four or eight times. You should feel more relaxed and refreshed, and you should feel clear and ready to start writing.

40

Face the tiger

Martial artists know that training in the *dojo* or *dojang* (the training hall) is only an approximation of what a real fight or combat situation will be like. They believe that training will help them cope with the real thing, but they don't pretend that training *is* the real thing. They may believe that they'll act a certain way if forced to defend themselves, but they can't know for certain until they've been forced to defend themselves. To be honest, most martial artists would prefer it never come to that.

But martial artists also know that chances are, at some point in their lives, they will be forced to face the real thing—the mugger or the rapist, the attacker who wants to hurt them. In other words, they will be forced to face the tiger. And they are much better prepared for it than the people who don't train to face the tiger, the people who believe the tiger will never wander into their neighborhood. Martial artists don't think that training encourages tigers to stop by. They think training helps them cope with the tigers who do drop by. They would much rather accept the fact of tigers than to pretend tigers don't exist when there's one sitting on the living room sofa, twitching its tail and waiting to pounce.

Warriors will face the tiger.

Writers have myriad methods to use to avoid facing the tiger—which in our case is putting ourselves and our writing out there in the world, putting ourselves on the line. We don't finish the novel, because if we do, we might have to submit it to publishers. We don't submit our poems to journals because they might get rejected. Only we don't say that, we say things like, "My work doesn't appeal to the masses," or "Those publications are run by people jealous of real writers." In other words, we give ourselves excuses for not facing the tiger. We let the idea of writing a novel—a big, long novel that will take a long time to finish—intimidate us so we never tackle it. We're certain the odds are stacked against us ever getting published, so why try?

As writers, we must face the tiger.

I'm sure some writers simply enjoy jotting down their words for their own entertainment. But most of us, honestly now, write because we want to communicate with other people. Because we have something to say, something to share. That means we have to put our work out there in order to be successful as writers. Not that we have to make a gazillion bucks or be published by a huge multinational publishing house to be writers. Just that we have to be out there.

Only by facing the tiger can you succeed as a writer.

Exercise

Face the tiger. Put yourself and your writing out in the world. Of course, facing the tiger when you're not ready isn't good for your survival, but writers often use that excuse to put it off for far too long. Give yourself a set time frame in which you will prepare yourself for facing the tiger (for example, writing the novel, getting a short story published). In that time—a month, six months, certainly no more than a year—gather all your tools and train as often as you can. Learn about the process of submitting work for publication so that your first excursion doesn't end in disaster because you handwrote your essay in purple ink. Read up on the craft of writing novels—read novels and read about writing novels every day or at least every week. But within your allotted time frame, face the tiger—write your novel, submit your short story, undertake the challenge.

41

Overcome fear by encountering it

Martial artists know that in a street fight, they'll be afraid. They'll be afraid of getting hurt, of getting maimed, of getting killed, so they train to learn how to handle this fear. They train to respond with a calm mind rather than a panicked one. They understand that adrenaline can affect their skills, so they train to expect that surge of adrenaline instead of letting it get in the way. Martial artists train to overcome fear by encountering it.

They participate in tournaments because doing a form in front of a panel of six or seven judges provokes fear. They know that stepping into a sparring ring against an opponent they've never seen before can evoke the panicked response of "Get me out of here!" They don't necessarily enjoy the tournament. They don't necessarily care if they win the tournament. They're there because it's good training. And after a while, it gets to be kinda fun in a masochistic sort of way.

Most martial arts styles require students to test as they make their way up the rank hierarchy. The martial artist must perform his techniques in front of an audience of judges (and an audience of onlookers). The martial artist fears not doing well, fears embarrassing himself. But the testing teaches him to focus only on the techniques he's performing at the moment. He learns to tune out the judges and the audience. He can't even hear them or see them after a while, he's so focused. By the time he's done a half dozen tests, they don't frighten him anymore. He has learned to control his fear by encountering it.

Writers can use this same tactic to overcome their fears. The more rejection letters you get, the less they hurt, the less you fear them. They don't really mean anything after a while except that you need to keep trying. When I first began writing, a rejection letter could ruin a whole day for me. But after frequent encounters with rejection letters, I stopped fearing them. They became simply pieces of information. Now I may have a few moments of disappointment, but that's all. I move on to the next thing on my to-do list and don't worry about it. You'll develop the same ability, too.

Exercise

Writers often overanalyze a situation in hopes of learning from it. You get a rejection letter and think, "What does this mean? What does this say about me as a writer? Does someone who knows recognize that I have no talent? Am I kidding myself?" This is fear talking. Ignore it. Don't overanalyze the rejection letter pile. A rejection doesn't mean that much. Editors and agents aren't gods who can tell from a quick glance at a query whether you'll thrive as a writer or not. You're the one who decides.

The next time you hear the voice of fear talking—"I could never win that award. I could never get published"—do it anyway. Apply for the award. Submit the manuscript for publication. It has worked for countless writers before and it will work for you.

42
The Way is not always straight

I had no intention of training in martial arts. I was on my way to the liquor store when my dissatisfaction with my life, my need to make meaningful changes, and a sign saying NEW HORIZONS BLACK BELT ACADEMY OF TAE KWON DO all collided together one summer afternoon, and the next thing I knew I was throwing people over my left shoulder.

Martial artists know the Way—the path, the journey— is not straight. No one enters the *dojo* (training hall) and moves serenely through the ranks to mastery. They encounter obstacles. They feel like giving up. They break an arm and have to listen to the doctor lecture them on how stupid it would be if they continued training. They keep on training regardless. Their instructor turns out not to be a person of integrity and courage, their school shuts down, they can't afford tuition this month or this year. They keep on training. Their favorite people leave the school, they get into a disagreement with the head instructor, they wonder what they're doing this for, and they keep on training. They get pregnant, they get sick, they get transferred—and they keep on training.

The Way is almost never straight.

This is true for writers as well. Writer Linda Formichelli points out, "Not every writer goes to journalism school, interns at a magazine, then moves to New York and starts writing for publication. I had just gotten my master's degree in Slavic linguistics and was working in a small office in Berkeley when I landed my first assignment." She had no formal training in writing but learned how to write a query (and run a writing business) by reading books about it. "Sometimes I wish I had taken a more direct route to writing," she says. "I could have started years ago and skipped college, grad school, and the nine-to-five grind, but I figure that my classroom experience and other jobs (more than twenty-five all told!) have contributed to making me the writer I am today."

Elia Kazan spent years directing plays and movies before turning his hand to fiction and seeing his novel land on the best-seller list. Dick Francis had a long career as a jockey before retiring at age thirty-seven; five years later he published the first of several dozen novels. Best-selling novelist Salley Vickers married, had children and pursued a career as a psychoanalyst before becoming a writer later in life. And Helen Hoover Santmyer, author of . . . *And Ladies of the Club,* was eighty-eight when her novel was published to wild success.

Exercise

Accept that you may not find the direct path to your writing dreams. Other people may seem to go directly from college to superstardom as a writer; be willing to go on with life if this is not you. Accept alterations in your plans. If you want to be a novelist and have the opportunity to do some business writing, go ahead and do the business writing. You never know where it may lead. Be open to the direction the Way is encouraging you to go and don't worry if it's not a straight path from point A to point B.

43

Catch sight of your reflection

In martial arts training sessions, much of the training focuses on the proper and perfect execution of techniques. While no one expects you to assume a perfect fighting stance when you're confronted by a mugger on the street, your instructor expects you to use one in the *dojo* (training hall). Martial artists practice their techniques through the performance of forms (*hyung* or *poomse* in Korean; *kata* in Japanese.) A form is a predetermined pattern of techniques, like a dance. Forms teach martial artists how to move from one technique to another, and they showcase the martial artist's balance, grace and agility.

When doing a form, you try to do each technique perfectly—correctly, quickly and powerfully. You try to make each stance the best stance you can. You try to imitate the moves of the senior students and your instructor. You try to feel how a good front stance uses different muscles from a back stance, and how a low block starts all the way up at your shoulder.

Most training halls have at least one or two walls with mirrors on them. By watching yourself in the mirrors, you can work on doing perfect techniques. Now and then, when you're performing a form, you may catch sight of yourself in the mirror—a revealing glimpse of how you look when you're doing your techniques. Sometimes it strikes you that you're beautiful when you do your form. Sometimes it strikes you that your front stances stink. In other words, when you catch sight of yourself, you can have good and bad reactions.

When you have a good reaction, that's terrific. You can feel confident about yourself. When you have a bad reaction, that's not so bad, really. If your front stances aren't as good as you thought they were, then that's something you need to know. It's something you can work on. (As one of my colleagues says, "That's why class is called *practice*, not *finished*.") The problem, the imperfection, was always there, and now that you know about it, you can do something to correct it.

As a writer, you can ask friends and colleagues and teachers to look at your writing and see what they think. You can hire freelance editors to tell you how you can improve your sentences and you can attend seminars on how to pump up your writing. But if you never learn to catch sight of your own reflection—that is, to see your own writing as it really is—you will never be able to improve as a writer. You'll never be as good as you could be.

Seeing your writing as it is can be daunting. You may want to cringe and say, "It's really not that bad, is it? This must be one of those funhouse mirrors that distorts the reflection." At the same time, you may feel embarrassed to say about your writing, "That was really beautiful. I nailed that sentence, that paragraph, that scene."

Learn to see your reflection. Don't get emotional about what you see. If you see that you have work to do, that's fine. That's even encouraging. There's something you can do to improve your writing, to increase your chances of success. Don't let the fact that you have work to do get you down. Let it become an opportunity to grow as a writer. At the same time, allow yourself to see those times when your writing rocks. It's just as important to your growth as a writer to find those beautiful reflections.

Exercise

See what your writing really looks like. Choose a time when you feel centered and strong, and feel ready to look at a piece of writing fairly.

Choose a piece of your own writing that you haven't looked at in a while—not the essay you were working on just yesterday. It should be something you don't have a stake in—it was published last year or it will never be published at all. Ask yourself, What works? What doesn't? Try reading aloud from the piece. This helps you "hear" how your language sounds. Do you stumble over sentences? Is it hard to follow your train of thought? It doesn't matter if you do find these problems. It doesn't mean you're a terrible writer. What matters is that you're seeing these problems now. And now that you see them, you can do something about them.

At the same time, don't just pillory yourself for your terrible writing. Find what's good in the piece. Maybe it has a great title. That's worthwhile. Maybe you nailed the conclusion. That's something many writers have trouble doing.

Do this once or twice a week until you start to have a realistic, reasonable sense of what strengths your writing possesses and what weaknesses it has. Then get to work perfecting your techniques.

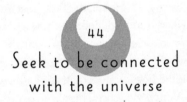

44
Seek to be connected with the universe

A martial artist learns that she is part of a history of connectedness—that she is related to other martial artists in the martial arts community, that she is linked to those who created and passed her style down through the generations and to those who will practice it in the future. She recognizes her part in this process, this network. She knows she has a place in the martial arts "family." As she grows in her understanding of the martial arts and the philosophies beneath them, she begins to understand the nature of the universe and her connection with it. She recognizes that she is not isolated and alone.

As a writer, staying connected to the universe is necessary to write in any meaningful way. You need to feel part of a network, a web. As a writer you work in isolation, but you can't be completely isolated or your work reflects your lack of connection to others, which means you cannot communicate effectively. So even though you may be tempted to shut down and shut out, you need to stay connected through your relationships with others, through your reading (of what others are reading), through your participating in the world around you.

Exercise

Writers must focus if they want to be successful, and sometimes this focus means excluding others from your life. While you may need to pare back your commitments so that you can devote yourself to writing, you also need to stay connected to the world—and the universe—around you.

Spend time out in the world on a regular basis. Sit in your front yard. Take the dog for a walk. Chat for a bit with your next door neighbor. Watch the sunset. Marvel.

45

Know when to yield and when to stand your ground

Entire martial arts styles are based on the idea that you can defeat your attacker by yielding to him. In other words, you use his energy against him. As he punches, you turn to allow the punch to slide by you. With a little flick of your wrist, you can send the attacker tumbling to the ground, owing to his own forward momentum. You didn't have to stand there and get pummeled. You yielded and defeated the attacker.

Most martial artists train with the understanding that some things are worth fighting over and some are not, and they spend time, effort and energy determining which is which. They realize that handing over their wallet is preferable to getting shot; ergo, the wallet is worth yielding. Conversely, they know that being shoved into the backseat of the getaway car means physical violence will occur, and so they stand their ground.

Writers must also navigate this territory. When should they yield, and when should they stand their ground? This question arises throughout a writer's career, as she determines which direction she'll take as a writer and which projects she'll pursue. It comes up when she has to decide which editorial comments will improve her writing, and which just tamper with it. The skill is in distinguishing when it's worth fighting over comma placement and when it's not.

Most professional writers, having experienced this question throughout their writing lives, develop guidelines that they may not consciously be aware of, but which correspond with their goals for themselves and their writing. They take the long view, which is that it rarely pays to jeopardize a business relationship by overreacting—to editing suggestions, to tasks they'd prefer not to do. At the same time, they're confident enough in their abilities to say, "No, I know this stuff and this sentence needs a comma." Beginning writers have a tendency to stand their ground when they would be better served by yielding; they can learn something from the process, and one thing they can learn is when it's imperative to stand your ground. (You find this out by yielding when you shouldn't have.)

Exercise

Develop your own guidelines about when to yield and when to stand your ground. For instance, it should be a no-brainer (but unfortunately sometimes it isn't) that you'll stand your ground when asked to do something immoral, unethical or illegal. You may not win any popularity contests, but at least you'll be able to live with yourself. If you write copy for business clients, remember that the client has the final say-so and if she wants to take the comma out, then out comes the comma. Yield, because that's what a professional does. Consider the painting contractor whose job it is to paint my living room, for example. He may advise me that the color I've chosen is too dark, but when I say I like it fine, his job is to paint the walls and bill me for his time, not dig his heels in and refuse to paint unless I choose a different color.

Come up with three or four questions or guidelines you can use to help you make business decisions that will result in writing success for you.

46

A warrior must be single-minded

When martial artists train, they have to focus on the training, not on what's for dinner. They know that if they're in a sparring match, they must be focused on winning the match. When they perform a form, they're not listening for applause, they're focused on doing the form to the best of their abilities. In other words, when the warrior does a task, she is single-minded about it. She doesn't get distracted part way through Won Hyo form and wander off to do some pushups. She completes the form as powerfully and as beautifully as she can . . . and she hates getting interrupted in the middle of it, which is why it's considered such poor etiquette to disturb a martial artist in the middle of training.

Writers must also be single-minded. So much competes for your attention that it's easy to get sidetracked and start doing the laundry, vacuuming, watching television or chatting on the phone with friends instead of writing. Other people will also put up obstacles to prevent you from achieving your goals. They may be well-meaning. "You work so hard, you deserve a break!" or not, "You don't really think you have enough talent, do you?" You may put up your own obstacles: "Who am I to take time away from my family/community/work/church/fill in the blank to pursue an egomaniacal desire to see my writing in print?" Some writers spend more energy on finding reasons not to write than on actually writing.

Being single-minded requires discipline. Sometimes you have to resort to drastic measures to ensure that you can stay single-minded. When it became obvious to me that I was spending way too much time watching television to the detriment of my career, I didn't even try to cut back on television viewing. I got rid of the television entirely. Do whatever it takes to stay focused on your writing goals.

Exercise

Explore what keeps you from being single-minded. Come up with ideas for keeping the distractions to a minimum. Of course you love your family and want to be with them, but it doesn't have to be every minute of every day. Perhaps if you set aside an evening a week to be there—wholly present and available for your family, focusing only on being with them—you'd fulfill your obligations to your family and still have time to write, instead of feeling guilty and abstracted and neither giving your full attention to your writing nor to your family. Perhaps work obligations impinge on your writing time. Make it a policy that after a certain time of day, the cell phone and the pager get turned off and anything that comes up will be dealt with the following day. You managed to muddle through somehow before cell phones and email; you'll figure out how to do it again. Be clear about what's distracting you, and come up with creative, workable solutions for staying focused.

47

Keep your power quiet

The martial artist who keeps his power quiet, like the martial artist who is humble, has an advantage over others. If he's attacked, the attacker won't be expecting the martial artist's skill and power—spelling defeat for the attacker. The martial artist who keeps his power quiet won't attract people who want to prove him wrong. He can save his energy and bruised flesh for more important things.

The martial artist who keeps his power quiet is not worried about gaining the adulation of the masses. He's not trying to attract hundreds of students, although he might have students. Instead, he focuses on becoming as powerful as possible in his own right, with the help and support of partners, teachers and students who want to see him succeed. Then, whenever necessary, he can use his power, confident and strong.

Writers can learn from this principle. Often, when you're successful, you attract envy and jealousy from others—less successful writers who strike out in spite, mean-spirited reviewers who can't stand to see someone enjoying a good reputation, wannabes who'll never actually write anything but who can't stomach anyone else succeeding. A writer who has achieved some success weathers this storm by remembering that her work has been published, that she is successful, that different people have different thoughts about what constitutes good writing.

It's not so easy for the aspiring writer to be exposed to this toxic environment. If you've never been published, and that nasty-tongued colleague in your writers' critique group repeatedly refers to the "superficial drivel" you write, it's a little hard to feel powerful about your work afterward. Sometimes it's the people you most care about who try to "protect" you by doing their best to annihilate your dreams. All in your best interest, of course, so that you won't get hurt by the rejection that will of course be your lot in life.

So it's important for a writer to protect herself (and her writing power, her creativity) from the people who would strangle it. That means only sharing dreams and aspirations with people you know you can count on, and not entrusting your fragile dreams to people who aren't worthy of the honor. If a friend or family member betrays you, then you will have to keep from giving them that power over you again. You will have to remain quiet about your writing hopes and goals. It may be difficult to do, but more than one bright writing career has been sidetracked by dream annihilators who will denigrate your work for the peculiar, twisted pleasure it gives them.

Which is not to say that many or most people will be planning mean things for you if you pursue your writing dreams. It just means that you keep your power quiet until you know if they'll support you.

Exercise

Seek support from people who will believe in you. More than anything, writers need to be nurtured. While getting editorial feedback on their work helps them grow as writers, what they really need is wholehearted support, especially among friends and family members. Beginning writers should establish a network of people who will be behind them 100 percent, who will encourage them through difficulties and who will be happy when they succeed. Remember, just because a person is a friend or is related to you by blood doesn't mean he or she will be your cheerleader, so choose your team wisely. Start slowly, by letting a few close friends know you're trying to become a writer. See what their reactions are. If they seem positive, go a step further with them. Share some ideas you've had about articles or short stories you'd like to write. Don't dump your beloved manuscript in the lap of the first person who expresses interest in your dreams. Use your judgment. Keep your power quiet. Let your supporters reveal themselves in their actions and behavior. Then allow them into your world.

48

Disharmony destroys focus

The martial artist knows that disharmony affects her ability to perform. If she's not feeling well (disharmony in her physical being), she won't be able to perform as usual. If she's feeling upset over an argument at work or with her lover (disharmony in her emotional being), she will have more difficulty concentrating on her training. With discipline, she will learn how to pull herself together to focus and perform despite disharmony, but it requires extra energy and effort to do so. If she can avoid the disharmony in the first place, she maintains focus more easily.

The martial artist seeks to find harmony and balance in all aspects of her life. Doing so allows her to remain focused and to feel strong and energized at all times.

Writers must develop balance and harmony to focus. Although some people believe that feeling emotional sparks their writing, over the long haul you can't sustain a high level of emotion without burning out. Being a productive writer is more easily accomplished if you're not constantly dealing with mangled emotions, tummy upset, and spiritual malaise.

After some years of training in the martial arts, I finally learned to let go of toxic relationships. I stopped hanging out with friends who were always utterly depressed no matter what happened, I stopped spending as much time with people who weren't supportive of my work, and I deliberately created a life conducive to writing. I only became close friends with people who were good for me. I learned to spend time and energy on relationships that were, in the long run, healthy and happy for me to be in. The result is far less conflict in my life. Not long ago, my agent mentioned how prolific I am, and how rare an attribute that is, and I said, "I am able to write all the time because I spend so little energy in conflict. I will engage in it if it's absolutely necessary, but it rarely is." This doesn't mean I suppress my feelings or frustrations; it means I simply don't spend a lot of time on the lesser emotions. My creativity is not spent yelling at an unsupportive spouse or a friend who denigrates my efforts. (I don't have either of those things in my life.) My creativity is spent writing. I work hard to keep harmony in my life and try to head disharmony off at the pass.

Exercise

Learn to spot disharmony. This is not as easy to do as it sounds. We get used to our relationships with people and don't realize how draining some of them can be. If you're avoiding your best friend when she calls, maybe it's because the friendship has changed from one of mutual support to something less harmonious. You may not need to abandon the friendship, but you may need to repair it. When you spot disharmony, set boundaries. It may not be practical, possible or desirable never to speak to your irascible father again, but you can limit what you talk about, and you can limit the amount of time you spend in his company. You can focus on what he does that's positive, and dwell less on what's negative. Sounds a bit optimistic? Give it a try. Back off a bit when you need to, consciously rid yourself of negative emotions, and focus on creating harmony throughout your life.

49

Let your intuition speak

To respond to threats effectively, martial artists move quickly and act immediately. They learn to sense a threat long before the first punch is thrown—and that's when self-defense can be most effective. In other words, they leave the room before the fists start flying.

Martial artists cultivate their intuition. They understand that at a basic, primal level, their animal instincts can tell them when a threat looms. Maybe it's just the way a person entering a room looks or smells. Maybe his expression reveals his discontent and anger and the martial artist senses he's looking for trouble. The wise martial artist slips away and doesn't oblige.

Of course, the martial artist has no way of knowing if he's right most of the time. He leaves the room and nothing happens; he walks back into the store and waits until the group of teenagers passes by and nothing happens; he decides to take the stairs instead of the elevator and nothing happens. He has no way of knowing whether his intuition and instincts are helpful. But he knows that when he doesn't listen to his intuition, he has lived to regret it.

A writer should cultivate her intuition as well. The writer who listens to her inner voice can make the right decisions about her career at the right time. It can help her decide who will be of aid to her career and who is more likely to be a hindrance. It can also help her decide which projects and partners to move forward with, and which to shy away from—at least until she has further information.

E x e r c i s e

Keep an intuition log, no matter how sappy it seems at first. When you get requests from clients, editors and other writers, take a moment to jot down what you're being asked to do and by whom, and how you feel about it. Listen to your intuition. Do you feel excited by the challenge, but afraid the person you're partnering with won't live up to expectations? Don't just dismiss your feelings. Use them as a basis for gathering more information before making a decision. Ask the person for referrals or samples of the work they've done before.

In my log, I also keep track of those times when something didn't work out for me—a co-author, a project, a publisher. I refer to this log if I'm ever tempted to work with that author, project or publisher again. I tend to be extremely optimistic that things will change for the better, and more than once I've been disappointed. My log reminds me to listen to my gut feeling, which is saying, "Oh, not again" even when I'm excited by the chance to do a new project or reach a new audience. The log helps me temper my first positive reaction and be more realistic about what I can expect to happen. Sometimes it'll be worth putting up with the co-author or publisher again, because it's the only way I can do a project I really want to do, or there's a lot of filthy lucre involved. In any case, the log helps remind me that I need to make changes in the relationship or set boundaries before going forward with it.

50

Don't give away your moves

Martial artists don't let everyone see all of their techniques all of the time. They save some of their moves for those times when they'll really need them—and then the techniques will be unexpected because the opponent will never have seen them before. If an opponent can be defeated in a sparring match using only five or six different techniques, then that's what the martial artist will do. He keeps additional techniques in reserve for different matches.

Some martial arts masters keep some of their techniques secret even from their highest ranking students, the theory being that if her students ever challenge her, she'll be able to defeat them because of these secret techniques she has practiced and sharpened but never shared.

Writers frequently give away all their moves. They share their experiences with each other, talk about how they got published, how they found their agent and any other detail of the writing life, and for the most part that's a good and generous thing to do. On the other hand, it has happened that one writer has stolen another's brilliant idea, perfect title, or terrific plot. So it pays to be careful before divulging all the details about what you're working on with others, at least until after you've got the contract all locked down.

But more importantly, talking about ideas and subjects can dissipate your interest in them and your passion and energy for pursuing them. After the twelfth time you've relayed the plot of the fabulous novel you're going to write someday, the impetus to actually write the thing has gone away. But if you keep quiet about details—"I'm working on a novel, and I hate to talk about work in progress, it changes so much"—then you won't steal your own thunder. Sure, you can occasionally consult other writers about a plot problem you're having and ask how they might solve it and sometimes talking about what you're working on can get you excited about it, but remember to be wise in how many details you dish and how often.

For Irving Wallace, this was a key to his writing success. In an article in *Writer's Digest,* he said, "You must want to write rather than be known as a writer. That's why you must treat your writing as a career. You must not talk about it. You must do it—want to do it, love to do it despite the loneliness, feel there is nothing more important on earth while you are doing it."

Exercise

Practice occasionally keeping your mouth shut, especially if you find that you do a lot more talking than actual writing. Instead of talking about a project, get started on it. This will help keep you from dissipating all your interest and enthusiasm in the project. If you're facing a challenge or having a problem you need advice for, by all means ask other writers (and readers) for their input. And certainly once you think you're ready to send your writing out into the world, it doesn't hurt to submit it to a critique group for feedback. But let your plots and characters percolate first . . . give yourself first crack at your ideas before you share them with others.

51

The Way shows itself differently for everyone

Martial artists seek to follow the Way—the path for creating balance in their lives, and attending to the needs of their minds, bodies and spirits. Martial artists have chosen one way, but they're not fooled into thinking it's the only way. Many other paths exist for people to meet their emotional and spiritual needs. The martial artist knows that while he finds the combat arts empowering and enlightening, not everyone will follow suit. Not everyone can.

Writers also find different Ways to their destination. In *Lesson #42: The Way is not always straight,* I talked about the Way in relationship to your writing career. Keeping focused on the journey (the Way) rather than the destination isn't important only for your writing career. It's important to understand it as part of the writing process, which is different for everyone.

I usually start my nonfiction with a basic outline—a table of contents—and let the writing build and add from there. I know what I want to include in the book, but where it goes and how it gets expressed is organic and constantly changing.

Many novelists start out with chapter by chapter plot outlines, while others begin with some characters and let them loose. Stephen King calls the writing process "finding the fossil," which tells you that he thinks of writing as a process of uncovering and discovering, not so much a process of building and adding. But each person finds his own process.

Many writers try to do what their favorite authors do. If their favorite novelist starts with a character and lets it speak, then that's what they do. If their favorite historian does three decades of research before setting pen to paper, then that's what they do. Instead, discover your own Way. Let your own writing process unfold for you instead of imposing preconceived ideas about how it should go. You can experiment with different approaches but once you find the process that works for you, stick with it. Don't feel you have to find something "better." If it works, it works. I have tried to map my books down to the final paragraph before starting to write, but find this robs me of most of the joy and entertainment of writing. It reduces what I do to filling in the blanks on a technical manual. But if I try to start with just a concept, without even outlining the bare bones, I get bogged down in trivia and sidetracked by unimportant details and descriptions. In other words, my in-between process works well for me. I may try a different approach now and then—especially for an unusual project—but I know what works just right for me and I usually follow it.

52
Protect the beginner

When a beginner starts training in martial arts, the instructor doesn't just throw him into the training hall to see if he sinks or swims. The instructor and the fellow students work with the beginner to help him learn the techniques and understand how to use them. They teach him how to protect himself and to keep from getting hurt. They teach him, in fact, how to be competition to them! By protecting the beginner, these martial artists know that they're cultivating what may someday be a good martial artist who will reflect well on the school, the system and them. If beginners don't come to train, the martial arts system dies out. That's not what anyone wants. That's why beginners are nurtured and protected—so they can carry on the martial art once they've gained competence and mastery of it.

Of course, not every beginner values the martial arts as much as the instructor and senior students might wish he would, and despite their best efforts, many beginners drop out. That's simply part of the process. Training in martial arts is not for everyone, but the martial arts instructor tries to make certain that it's not his teaching that turns the student off.

As writers, we must also protect the beginners among us, although it's fashionable to put them down and roll our eyes at 'em. They have energy, enthusiasm and fearlessness that can inspire us. Caring about beginners reminds me that my success is a great gift and to value it. Recently, all the demands on my time were stacking up and I told my agent, "I quit. I'm going back to unloading trucks for a living." The next day, I gave a workshop for aspiring writers. I didn't tell them I had quit. Their interest in hearing how I'd achieved success and their desire to have a life like mine reminded me of how fortunate I am. So I called my agent and said, "Okay, I'm staying."

Veteran writer Linda Formichelli always makes time for the beginners who contact her: "Once I became successful, aspiring writers started contacting me for advice. I always remember a couple of things: one, that someone helped me out when I was getting started and now I have a chance to help someone else, and two, that if I help a beginner, she will probably help me out someday by putting me in contact with her editors and sharing her leads with me." Linda goes on to report, "Recently, a new writer asked me to critique her query. I did, and she sold the idea to *Parents* magazine! Another writer e-mailed me to say that she used the information from my Newbie Writer FAQ webpage to sell her first three articles. I know what it's like to jump into the scary world of freelancing, and I'm very proud to have helped these writers get their start."

Protecting and nurturing the beginner helps the beginner and the master.

Exercise

If you're an aspiring writer, you need to be protected and nurtured, and it's okay to ask for it! Not everyone will want to help you out, but some will. Connect with writers through local writers' groups, and mine their experiences for information that will help you. If you're a more established writer, make it a point to mentor those coming along behind you. Yes, they're your competition, but if you help them, they can also be your colleagues—they may be the ones sharing leads with you someday down the road.

53

Do what is right

Since martial artists learn physical techniques and methods of fighting that can be pretty dangerous to average Joes, they must follow guidelines for using their skills. For example, to use one's knowledge of martial arts to attack another person is wrong, under any circumstances. Martial arts should only be used for defensive purposes. Martial artists also know that, because of their skills, they're obligated to help those who can't take care of themselves. In other words, it's not okay to walk away when you see a child being hurt. You don't get to ignore the scene when a person who can't fight back is being attacked. You have to do what is right, even if it's difficult and you have other things to do.

In your writing life, it's also important to do what is right. In *Lesson #27: Your beliefs guide your strategy,* I described how your personal beliefs should guide your writing career. Now, I'm referring to professional ethics—questions such as being fair in what you write, not exploiting people you work with or who work for you, even if you can. Doing what is right as a matter of professional ethics means if you agree, in principle, to contract terms, you don't suddenly start renegotiating them when the contract arrives. It means being generous and fair to subcontractors and others involved in your work. In other words, your professional writing life should embody the principle of doing what is right.

Exercise

Educate yourself on professional standards. Know how professional journalists and writers conduct themselves. Find out what is considered ethical versus unethical behavior for a writer. In some cases, you'll see gray areas. (For example, is it okay to "spruce up" an interviewee's quotations to get rid of all the "er"s and "um"s and circular statements? Or must you present the quotation exactly as you jotted it down, even if it makes the interviewee sound a bit stupid?) You need to decide what standards you'll follow, and you'll need to understand what standards the organizations you write for follow. (For example, some magazines have a policy of allowing sprucing up as long as the gist and the general wording of the quotation remain the same; others won't allow any tampering with quotes.) Do your homework and pledge to maintain professional standards in all your writing.

54

Choose the path; never look back

When I began training in martial arts, it meant a whole new life for me. It meant I gave up smoking and cut back on drinking and watched what I ate and worked out every night. All of these were good things and I felt positive about them. It was just that sometimes I missed the old life. I missed loafing around in the evenings instead of working out. I missed scarfing down a huge tub of buttered popcorn while watching the matinee. All this being good to myself was sometimes, frankly, a little restrictive. I'd sling my gear bag over my shoulder on my way to train, and I'd lock the front door, thinking how much fun it would be just to put my feet up, pop open a wine cooler and chat with friends.

This tendency to look back on the way my life used to be and to wax nostalgic about it nearly derailed my martial arts training before it got off the ground.

I related this challenge to one of the black belts early in my training, and she looked at me and said, "Stop looking back."

Just that. Made perfect sense to me. I had chosen a new path, and it was time to look forward, to see where it was leading me, instead of focusing on where it was taking me from.

The same holds true for writers. Once you've chosen the path—you've committed to being a writer and you have a plan for making it come true—don't look back. Don't think about how much easier it was before you started devoting your evenings to writing. Think only about how the time spent writing is rewarding and enjoyable now and will yield even greater rewards for you in the future.

In other words, once you've chosen the path (or it has chosen you), concentrate on the present and let the past go.

Exercise

The best way to stop second-guessing yourself and wondering if you should have taken a different fork in the road is to focus on your goals and the steps you're taking to get there, says goal guru Bev Bachel. Devise a plan for the writing path you're on and think positively about the things you can do in the present and the future to achieve your goals. Focusing on these goals helps you forget how comfortable it might be to do something else. Being able to see your forward progress helps you keep from looking back and wondering if a different strategy would have been better.

55

Someone else's win is not always your loss

In a martial arts competition, someone wins and someone loses. One martial artist scores more points than the other. One martial artist's form garners higher praise than another. Clearly, there's a winner and a loser. Or is there? If you're competing with other martial artists, someone else's win is not always your loss. In other words, sometimes you learn enough from the competition that your final score is immaterial. The simple fact of competing in the tournament may be a victory for you if you've never competed before. Just doing your form in front of judges, even though you're sweating and nervous and your heart's in your mouth, can be an unqualified success even if you don't place. And sometimes, if you've been training with a partner and trying to help him become better, his victory over you is a victory *for* you, too, because you helped make it happen.

In writing, it can be hard to see someone else "win" and not feel like a loser in comparison. Because the business is highly competitive, writers sometimes get frustrated or disheartened when others seem to achieve more than they. A college-age writer scores a big advance for a first novel, while the experienced, polished novelist struggles to get mediocre advances. Or a non-writer gets a huge advance because something happened in her life that catches the media's attention. Through no effort of her own, she seems to have won the publishing lotto.

Anne Lamott says in *Bird by Bird*, "Of all the voices you'll hear . . . the most difficult to subdue may be that of jealousy. Jealousy is such a direct attack on whatever measure of confidence you've been able to muster. But if you continue to write, you are probably going to have to deal with it, because some wonderful, dazzling successes are going to happen for some of the most awful, angry, undeserving writers you know—people who are, in other words, not you."

I'm no stranger to this feeling. I remember turning green with envy a few years ago when one of my sisters told me that an editor was extremely interested in her novel. My sister figured I was one of the few people she knew who understood how exciting that news was. I actually thought, "I will kill myself if she gets a novel published before I do." Not something I'm exactly proud to admit.

More recently, one writer whom I advised turned my advice into the biggest contract a certain publishing company had ever offered. I had to swallow a faint, "Why not me?" when she excitedly told me the news.

But the truth is, just because these writers "won," it didn't mean I had somehow lost. They could win and I could win, too. Their victory is mine as well.

Exercise

If a writer has gotten something you legitmately want for yourself, put the feeling of "Why not me?" to good use. Instead of seething with jealousy, redouble your efforts toward getting published yourself or developing a platform that will earn you bigger advances, or coming up with an idea for your next novel that'll knock their socks off.

56
Accept criticism to grow

If a martial artist shows up and trains every single day, and her instructor never comments on her techniques, neither praising them nor criticizing them, will she grow and improve as a martial artist? Probably not. She may be able to observe what others are doing, and try to emulate them, but until and unless an outside party more experienced than she herself coaches her, she will never reach her full potential.

In other words, she has to listen to criticism to grow. She has to learn what she's doing wrong in order to learn how to do it right.

Writers also have to accept criticism to grow, although it can be extremely painful to listen to it. We're humans, so we try to avoid pain when we can. But as food writer and hospitality consultant Jennie Schacht says, "I couldn't possibly get it right without the support and assistance—including criticism—of my colleagues in my writing group."

Certainly, sometimes a reader criticizing your work clearly doesn't get it, wasn't paying much attention or has another axe to grind. (Someone once told me about a novel I was working on, "I hate artists as narrators," a criticism I immediately filed in the circular file.) Understand that sometimes you'll get chaff, instead of helpful, usable information about your writing. But other times, you will get wheat, and you'll develop a sense of where your story drifts off-track or why you're losing your audience when you begin the argument about why Tae Kwon Do is better than Karate.

Keep in mind that while experienced writers have a writer's eye and can help you out one way, aspiring, inexperienced writers can bring a reader's eye to your work, which is equally as valuable.

Exercise

Join a critique group to grow as a writer. This can be something informal, such as arranging with a friend to read her stuff if she'll read yours. Or it can be more formal, like a group that meets at someone's home once a month and trades off stories to read and critique. It could be a class at a local arts center or community college. Put the word out among your friends and family members, and you'll be able to find a supportive critique group that will help you grow.

57

You can do more than you believe possible

The first time the instructor said to me, "For your blue belt test, you need to learn the jump spinning wheel kick," which required me to jump high in the air, spin backward, and strike a board with my heel, I laughed myself silly. I stopped laughing as soon as I realized the instructor was serious. "I'm sorry," I seem to recall saying, "but I'm afraid I will never be able to perform that kick."

It won't surprise you to learn that with this attitude, it took me something in the neighborhood of seven years to learn how to do the kick. I did a reasonable facsimile of it for my blue belt test, and passed, but I knew, and the instructor knew, that I could do better. Finally, one day—this was after I had earned my black belt—I finally sprang into the air, spun to the back and broke the board with a sharp satisfying crack.

I am sure there are plenty of people who could think of better ways to spend their time, but the point is, you can do more than you believe possible. I certainly never entertained the notion that that kick was possible until I actually did it. Then suddenly it was easy. Imagine if I had believed it was possible before I started practicing it.

Writers should also know that by pushing themselves they can achieve far more than they thought possible. It may seem that publication is out of your reach or that you'll never be able to write a novel. You may feel you'll never be able to sustain a freelance career. You may believe that people younger, more talented, more connected than you could achieve those things, but you yourself—nah, not going to happen.

Of course, this is wrong. You can do more than you thought possible. You may not have the ability or capacity today or this week but you will eventually if you keep striving toward it.

Exercise

Make a list of those things you think you'll never be able to achieve in your writing career. Be as pathetic or bathetic as you like, and list everything that comes to mind. Now, zero in on the beliefs that are holding you back—such as, "I'll never get published so why bother trying?" Reframe these as possibilities. "If I keep trying, I will get published." If necessary, make a list of things you've accomplished that you never thought you would, no matter how seemingly inconsequential—you refinished a cabinet, you learned to knit, you speak passable French. Use these as reminders that anything is possible.

58

Hone unexpected skills

The more skills martial artists possess, the more likely they'll be able to defend themselves. They learn to use their hands and feet to protect themselves, they learn to use weapons, including those lying around the house such as baseball bats and letter openers. They learn to use their voices as a weapon. Occasionally, the martial artist develops a physical skill that's unexpected. He can do spectacular leaping kicks, for example. I developed an unexpected knack for punches, which is unusual in my style, as it relies on kicking techniques. Others learn joint manipulation or trapping techniques to redirect an attacker's energy. Any or all of these skills may have a direct bearing on the martial artist's eventual survival.

As a writer, an unexpected skill can make you more valuable and prove quite lucrative. If you have a natural turn of phrase that makes ordinary advertising copy look lifeless and pale by comparison, don't discount the skill. It's worth quite a lot to the right people.

For myself, I learned that I was a pretty decent photographer and started illustrating my own books. This made me more valuable as a writer on any project. The editor and publisher could always rest assured that I'd get the illustrations needed no matter what.

Bob Spear is a guitar player and storyteller. He writes children's stories, then goes around to local schools with his singing-and-reading show. He's a huge hit and he's responsible for turning lots of children on to reading.

Samantha Clark, an artist who can no longer paint owing to hand injuries, teaches writers how to use an artist's eye in their work—and uses her own artist's eye in her writing. By tapping into an unexpected skill, these writers and many others have experienced success in their writing careers.

Being a successful writer requires a wide range of skills. Hone any natural talents, abilities or aptitudes you have whether you think they'll be worthwhile in the long run or not. A writer of non-fiction who is an expert in a subject matter, whether it's snowy egrets or NFL athletes, can do well. One who can write press releases in no time flat is useful not only to clients but to herself when she publicizes her own work. Don't sell your talents short. See how you can incorporate them into your writing career.

59

Focus on the openings

When a martial artist spars, he looks for the openings in his opponent's guard. For example, when the opponent leans back to deliver a kick and in doing so exposes his ribs, the martial artist sees the opening, strikes to it, and scores a point. He takes advantage. He doesn't wait until the next time an opening becomes available. He doesn't think, "My partner doesn't know what he's doing, so I'll give him a break this time."

A writer must also take advantage of the openings. But unlike the martial artist, sometimes the writer doesn't realize the openings are actually openings. For example, if you send an article query and the editor writes back saying, "We can't use your idea because we have enough feature articles. Right now, we're looking for product roundups," that's not a rejection, that's an opening. But all too often the only thing the writer can see is the rejection and not the opening. A smart writer would fire off another letter to the editor saying, "Thanks for your recent response to my letter about child-proofing the kitchen. You said you were looking for round-up articles, so perhaps you'd be interested in a product roundup featuring safety products for infants and young children?" The less successful writer would throw the rejection letter on the rejection letter pile and wonder where he should send his query next.

Exercise

Take an inventory of all the possible writing work you could do right now, whether for pay, or barter, or to get in good with the boss. Consider the people you know and where they work and what their personal needs are. Be creative and use your imagination to consider various projects you could do. Look in *Writer's Market* or another market guide for an idea of the different types of writing projects writers can become involved in. Think about small presses that publish poetry and fiction. Don't overlook on-line sites. In other words, try to find openings for your writing and pursue them.

60
Draw out the guard

When a martial artist spars an opponent, he doesn't just have to sit and wait patiently for openings to come his way. He can draw out the guard. That is, he can fool the opponent into letting down his guard, thus creating an opening. He can draw out the guard by pretending to strike to one target (so that the opponent will automatically move to block the strike) while actually aiming for a different target (one that is now exposed because the opponent took the bait and tried to block a strike that never happened). Feints and jabs work to create openings. Lures also work, too, where the martial artist deliberately lets down his guard, hoping to draw the opponent into a foolish action.

Writers can take this approach to heart, too. They can use their skills and techniques to create openings where none existed before. For example, maybe you can convince your boss that your company needs a newsletter, and you'd be happy to edit it. With that in your portfolio, you can seek additional, related work from other corporations you want to freelance for. Get friendly with a freelance graphic designer and ask her to send referrals your way when a business owner asks if she knows any good copywriters. Join the local Chamber of Commerce and attend the next mixer, letting everyone you meet know that you're a commercial writer.

I once joined the staff of a university literary magazine. I was under the impression that such a vehicle must be deluged with stories to choose from, with all those aspiring writers walking the halls. Not so. Every issue, we had to make a desperate attempt to fill up the pages, soliciting work from friends, fellow students, anyone we could pound a couple thousand words out of. Had I known this as an undergraduate, you can be sure I would have submitted my sterling prose from time to time. So don't assume that a market is too tough to crack just because it appears to be. Give it a try, find out more about it, and create your own openings.

Exercise

Focusing on the type of writing you want to do, consider some ways to draw out the guard and create openings where none existed before. Suppose you're partial to short stories. Beyond the usual submitting to journals, what can you do to get some attention for your work? Maybe you could approach the local newspaper and suggest they hold a talent contest for short story writers. (Unless you live in New York, local newspapers often listen to what their readers and subscribers think are good ideas.) Maybe you could join a writers' organization and suggest that some part of each local newsletter be devoted to publishing the work of its members. Maybe you could write short stories for gifts. Maybe you could sell "your name here" short stories where clients suggest names and plot details and you write to order, the client then giving the short story as a gift or enjoying it himself. (Hey, this worked for me in high school, when I wrote short stories featuring my friends and their current crushes doing all the fun and romantic things they'd never do in real life.)

61

Do not be surprised when the scorpion stings

A story that often gets told in the martial arts has to do with a scorpion promising not to sting a hippo if the hippo will help him get across the river. The hippo agrees to give the scorpion the help he needs, but halfway across the river, the scorpion stings the hippo (you knew that was coming), thereby destroying them both. As they drown, the hippo asks why the scorpion had to go ahead and sting him, dooming them both, and the scorpion says, "It is the nature of the scorpion to sting."

The moral of this story, at least in martial arts terms, is that someone who has caused trouble in the past is likely to cause trouble in the future, no matter how much he claims to have changed. So it is in your best interest to be very wary of such people. In other words, belligerent drunks sooner or later start throwing things, so when the belligerent drunk shows up at the party, it's time for you to leave.

In the same way, if a sparring partner always kicks below the belt when you partner with him, no matter how much you complain, the next time you're paired up with him, you can be pretty sure you're going to take a hit or two below the belt. It makes sense, then, to change your strategy so that he doesn't get in range of your belt or vicinities south. In other words, you can alter your own behavior much more easily than you'll ever alter the scorpion's.

Writers need to understand that it is the nature of publishing that bad things happen—that the scorpion stings. It isn't a matter of *if* you'll get stung, it's a matter of *when*. But if you fear the sting too much—so much that you don't risk it—you'll never enjoy the privilege and benefits of being a writer. Expect to get stung, expect it will hurt a lot, learn something from it and get on with your writing career. Assume that even though the magazine editor has asked to look at an article on speculation, you won't sell it. Expect that even though you've gone through the enormous difficulty of finding an editor who loves your book and tries to sell it to the editorial committee, the publisher will veto the manuscript and you'll be out cold. Or that even if your book is published, it will sell only three hundred copies before being remaindered. These setbacks and disappointments will happen—and the more you're out there, the more they'll happen—but being prepared makes all the difference.

Exercise

Knowing the scorpion stings can help you avoid it, too, by always maintaining professional standards and by creating a step-by-step plan to reach your writing goals. If you know what steps you need to take to get where you want to go, you simply keep following those steps until you achieve success. If, for example, you're prepared for the possibility that your book could sell only three hundred copies, you can create a plan to promote it in order to sell more. If you know that you need an agent to market your novel to publishers, be prepared for an agent who takes your manuscript on—but doesn't end up selling it. In other words, give that agent only one project and a specific amount of time in which to sell it (perhaps six months or a year). Being prepared can help you achieve your writing goals.

62

Practice daily, regardless of circumstances

One of the commitments a martial artist makes when she begins her study is to train daily, regardless of circumstances—regardless of what else happens in her life. She may or may not make it to the *dojo* (training hall) every single day, but she trains every single day. She may, as one of my friends does, practice her forms in her head before falling asleep every night. If that's the only possible practice she can get in, it's better than nothing.

The commitment to practice despite circumstances means that the training will take priority over other things. It means you'll squeeze it in even though you do have work and family obligations. It means you carve out a specific amount of time to train every day, no matter if you're sick, been transferred to Timbuktu, or inherited eight million dollars.

Writers must do the same. Because we have so much to distract us (even those of us who make our living as writers have lots of things to distract us), we often blame our circumstances when we don't get our books and articles written. But making the commitment to practice daily means we don't let those excuses win out. We simply make sure that every day, we do some writing.

Who hasn't heard the story of J. K. Rowling, the impoverished single mother of a toddler, scribbling away at the cafe table, trying to get the first Harry Potter book written? If she can manage to write a terrific novel during her daughter's naps, so can you.

Exercise

If you have trouble finding the time to write, make writing in your journal a ritual just before you go to bed (or first thing in the morning, before you jump in the shower). Just make it part of the plan, like brushing your teeth and changing into your pajamas. Soon you'll find yourself wanting, scheduling and getting more time to write. And you'll keep your promise to yourself and write at least ten minutes a day, no matter what.

63

Commit to training

The martial artist knows that to master the techniques, he has to commit to training. This means daily practice, of course, but it also means dedicating himself to learning all he can about the martial arts. In other words, it's one thing to show up and work out every afternoon—any aerobics aficionado can do this, and it doesn't make him a warrior—and it's another thing to commit to training, to dedicate oneself to learning and mastering the skills.

The writer has to be committed to training in just the same way. He must be a lifelong learner. He must never be so sure that he's got it all figured out that he can't listen to a new idea or try a new way of doing things.

When you commit to being a writer, you commit to learning the craft. Even though I've been doing this for a number of years, each new book is an opportunity for me to be better than before. Each new editor can show me something more about the craft, if I'm willing to listen. With each new book proposal, I learn something new from my agent—or have something old reinforced. Knowing I'm not totally confident with my magazine articles, I ask a trusted friend who writes articles for a living for her help and advice. In turn, when she puts together a book proposal, she asks me to give feedback. I even learn something from my failures. When a book proposal is rejected by the publishers my agent and I send it to, we try to determine what the problem was. We've always successfully identified the cause or causes of rejection and know better for next time.

E x e r c i s e

At least once a month, expose yourself to an "educational opportunity" in some aspect of writing. Attend a workshop, read a book, have a leisurely chat with a friend who has more experience than you do or who works in a different field. Be willing to spend time and money on training—it's probably tax deductible and will repay itself later multiple times.

64
Strive for mastery

The martial artist knows that once he has done the front kick one hundred times a day for three years that he has a pretty good front kick and it will serve him well should he ever need to use it in a fight. But that doesn't mean he stops practicing the front kick, or that he thinks it's as good as it's ever going to get, or that he believes all he has to do is maintain his skill level instead of trying to improve it. The martial artist continues to strive for mastery even when he's pretty darned good at what he does, even when he has students of his own, even when his students have students of *their* own. Most martial artists agree that they can never reach the peak of perfection and attain perfect mastery, but they try anyway. Because the striving for mastery is the whole point, in a way that learning techniques for self-defense never can be, at least beyond a certain stage.

After a period of concentrated effort, writers can achieve a certain level of competency that will result in satisfied clients and sales to publications. But if they never try to go beyond that level of competency, they sell themselves short. If they never explore different voices, different media, different types of writing, they limit themselves to just a small sampling of what the world can offer writers.

A writer should strive for mastery even if she's experienced, even after she has won prestigious awards, even when she's earned the acclamation of her peers. At no point should she be completely satisfied with her work. To do so, to think it will never get better than this, is the first step toward decay and eventual loss of writing power.

Exercise

Occasionally, don't settle for competent work—the copy you turn in to make clients happy, the manuscript you ship off to your publisher certain that it does its job. Take the time to review the writing, to re-envision it, take it apart and re-assemble it, get feedback from colleagues and actually listen to and incorporate their thoughts and comments. Really fiddle with the piece until you've hopelessly screwed it up (in which case you revert to the saved copy of the original) or you have something that is truly finer than your usual product. Seeing that you can attain a very high level in your writing should inspire you to reach for it more often.

65

No one gets the jump spinning wheel kick on the first try

As I alluded to in *Lesson #57: You can do more than you believe possible,* when I was first shown the jump spinning wheel kick, I knew I'd never get it. I eventually did, of course, or I wouldn't have brought it up as an illustration of *You can do more than you believe possible.* But I certainly did not get it on the first try, or on the fifteenth or on the fiftieth. After hanging around martial arts schools for long enough, I realized that *no one* gets the jump spinning wheel kick on the first try, no matter how athletic they are, or how young they are, or if they have the jump gene (which I, lamentably, do not). No one gets it on the first try, not even athletes skilled in other physical techniques. For some probably despicable reason, this gives me great satisfaction. I think I like the idea that there are still some things you have to learn—that you have to earn. You can't go out and buy a jump spinning wheel kick the way you apparently can the presidency, no matter who your parents are.

Writing is like that, too. No one gets it right on the first try. Some come closer than others, and some delude their agents and editors into thinking they have, but the fact is, no one gets it right on the first try, and that should comfort you just as much as it comforts me.

Practically no one who gets a first novel published (or a debut novel, as we're calling them these days) actually gets a first novel published. It's usually their fifth novel or the twelfth. It's just the first one anyone saw fit to publish, all the ones that went before it being unworthy of the shelves at Borders.

E x e r c i s e

Accept that you will spend months, maybe years, in your apprenticeship as a writer. During this period, you may not let anything see the light of day, or if you do, you may find that none of it gets published, or very little of it gets noticed. That's okay. That's the way of being a writer. Remember that one fine day all those months and years of learning the craft will finally come to fruition and you'll achieve the success you've longed for. But there's no need to rush it—in fact, it really can't be rushed. Each writer reaches her potential according to her own path, and according to an unknowable timetable, so just be patient and it will come for you, too.

66
Find your passion

Martial artists are taught using a variety of approaches. There's the repetitive practice of kicks and punches and throws. There's the performance of forms—patterns of movements like a dance. There's some form of mock combat, such as sparring. There may be added attractions like board breaking. Depending on one's style, several of these approaches will be combined to form the core lessons of training. A martial artist is expected to practice each approach faithfully, but every martial artist finds the one approach he or she feels most passionate about, and tends to spend more time on it. As with any type of learning, some of us learn better in one way than another, and the various approaches help us find the way we can learn best.

The approach a martial artist prefers tells you a lot about the martial artist. One of my friends is a forms nut. She can do every form she ever learned (dozens of them) backward, forward, reverse, according to count ("Do the sixth move of Choryo form. Now the seventh move of Dan Gun"), eyes closed, mirror image, practically any variation you could think of. She demonstrates balance, agility and power when she does her forms.

Me, I get too many senior moments performing forms

to adore the darned things. ("What do I do next? Oh, yeah, low block, middle punch. Now what?") I'm not so fabulous with the repetitive practice of kicks. My friends kindly call my tornado kick a "stiff wind kick." But I am wicked when it comes to sparring. I'm faster than anyone looking at me would believe possible, I'm savvier than most people I spar, and I can get my backfist in on any opponent I've ever faced. I love sparring. I love how I can see the opening before it arrives and take what seems to me all the time in the world—but which is really a microsecond—to strike to it. Nothing else is ever happening in the world when I'm sparring. And when I'm done, I take a lot of pleasure in counting up my bruises. So that's my passion. I don't care how good forms are for me to do, they'll never replace how I feel about sparring.

As a writer, you, too should find your passion. There are many ways to see your words in print, many approaches you can take, but if you find your passion, you'll be able to commit to your writing and stick with it even during the difficult times.

My friend Mary O'Connell loves to write short stories. She's capable of other types of writing, of course, but short stories are really her forte. Of course, as everyone has been told, collections of short stories never sell . . . do they? Apparently that "truth" doesn't always hold because after several of her short stories were published in literary journals, an agent approached her about putting a collection together, and the collection sold to a large publisher for what they call in the trade "a nice sum." Following her passion paid off for Mary.

Exercise

You may think you know what your passion is, but give yourself the opportunity to explore. You may find that you feel passionate about other subject matters or modes of writing, which will afford you more opportunities for success. But if one particular approach really turns you off and it's worse than cleaning teeth for a living to do, don't pursue that angle no matter how good at it you may be. I gave up editing for pay because it made me bang my head against the wall in frustration, even though I could get freelance jobs and I was pretty good at it. Same with PR writing. Now the only PR writing I will do is for my own projects, because then I don't mind putting together good copy for myself, and I don't feel like anyone else cares about my work as much as I do. Follow your passion to your writing success.

67

Heart is more important than talent

Commonly, two types of people enroll in martial arts schools. One type is the young, already athletic individual interested in new physical and mental challenges. This person believes his body can do anything, has demonstrated it, and has plenty of raw talent, aptitude and ability. The other type is the person who has arisen from the sofa just long enough to trot to the corner martial arts academy because it's something she has always wanted to do, but just never had the x to do it: x = courage, money, lack of other obligations, proximity to a teacher.

Sometimes members of the first category have as much heart as they have talent. They love martial arts, they love the techniques, they're driven to master them, and they do (it helps that they're gifted with physical skills and abilities the rest of us mortals can only sit and envy). But often, more often than you would think, members of the first category have talent but no heart. They wash out long before ever reaching black belt. They've moved on to the next thing.

Members of the second category, on the other hand, rarely display much in the way of innate physical talent. Everything they learn, they learn it the hard way. Every technique takes them ten thousand repetitions to figure out. When they begin training, you look at them and wonder if they ever realized they had a physical body before.

Sometimes the people in category two are just trying martial arts out to see if it fits, and they give it a go, realize it's more demanding than they're prepared for, and they toddle off to their sofas. But frequently, more frequently than you would think, members of this second category have more heart than you can measure. They love martial arts. They love martial arts, and training in the martial arts, and learning everything the hard way. They love it more than chocolate or movies. They will do anything, including ten thousand repetitions, to get it.

And they are the ones who achieve their black belts.

The same holds true for writers. Heart trumps talent. Yes, it helps if you have a way with words. But more important is your willingness to learn the craft and to persist despite obstacles. Every aspiring writer has looked at a published book, maybe even a popular, best-selling book, and said, "I can do this!" Or "I can do *better* than this!" But the fact is, the ability to write, even the ability to write better than a best-selling novelist, is only part of the equation. Writing success depends more on heart (belief in yourself, perseverance) than on talent.

Harlan Ellison says, "Writing is the hardest work in the world . . . it is dangerous. It demands courage and heart." Courage and heart. These are more important than talent.

Exercise

Remember that talent will only take you so far, and that you need heart to see you the distance in your writing career. If you don't really care about writing—you only do it because people think you're good at it—you might be better off finding a less difficult way to make a living. But if you want to write because you'd shrivel up and die if you didn't, you're on the right track. Focus on maintaining an upbeat attitude about your writing in spite of any difficulties you may encounter. Love what you do. Admit it into your life and embrace it. This passion—this heart—will see you through.

68

Observe without judging

Martial artists learn from other martial artists all the time. They watch how others spar, and see what techniques their competitors select for their board breaks. They attend workshops in other styles to see what they can glean from them. But if the martial artist approaches her observation with a judgmental attitude, she won't learn as much as possible. In other words, if she's predisposed to believe that grappling styles are naturally inferior to striking styles, it's not likely she'll get much out of the Jujitsu seminar she takes. On the other hand, if she observes without judging—if she takes the information in and sees if it can apply to her own talents and aptitudes—she's more likely to learn something she can benefit from.

Writers who observe the world around them without automatically judging or condemning what they see can create worlds that seem realistically drawn and which invite readers in. Allowing the reader to make her own judgment is a powerful skill, one that few writers use effectively. This technique might be called *observe-and-report* without judging.

The technique of observing without judging applies to your writing life beyond craft. If you observe what other writers do without judging ("I would never do that! Such shameless self promotion!") you can see what's effective in a writing career and maybe even emulate strategies that in your first judgment you would have disregarded without further thought.

Exercise

Record the people, sights and events you encounter over a period of a few days. Make a concentrated effort to simply observe and record. Instead of using your judgment when writing, merely describe what you see ("older woman in curlers wearing a printed pink dress starts arguing with the clerk at Wal-Mart over the price of a bag of pork rinds"). Flex your descriptive muscles instead of your judgmental ones. ("Some looney tunes starts bitching about the price of junk food" doesn't bring the same mental image to mind.) See how quickly this observation without judgment translates into more powerful prose.

69
Know yourself

It doesn't come as any surprise to my sparring partners that I'm going to try to score a point using my patented backfist strike to the temple. It doesn't come as any surprise to me, either, because I know myself. In martial arts training, martial artists learn to know themselves, their tendencies, their strengths and their weaknesses. Martial artists learn about themselves so they can shore up their weaknesses before an opponent or attacker can exploit them. They must learn to capitalize on their strengths so that said opponent or attacker never gets a chance to prey on their weaknesses. You'd think that the people I spar, expecting the backfist, would be able to defend themselves against it. And sometimes they can. But the fact is, I've figured out how to get around practically any defense against it. I've had one or two sparring partners look at me just before the match and say, "Why don't you just go ahead and do that backfist now since I know you're going to anyway?"

People who spar me know that just as I always use the backfist, I never use the crescent kick in sparring. I know I never use the crescent kick. That's my weakness. A good way to beat me at sparring is to get me into situations where I need to use a crescent kick. But since I know myself—my strengths and my weaknesses—I almost never let an opponent work me into a position where I need to use the crescent kick.

Writers need to know themselves, too. They need to play to their strengths and shore up their weaknesses. If I know my strength is snappy dialogue, then maybe a slow-paced literary novel with scads of room for descriptive passages should not be my first choice for writing fiction. Instead, I could chose a plot-driven format where the snappy dialogue gives the impression of character without a lot of painful digression to discuss why Joe has such a hard-hearted attitude toward Linda. A reader picking up such a novel would appreciate its merits and would not expect a lot of painstaking character development. Which doesn't mean I shouldn't work on character development. It just means I should put my best side forward.

If I know my weakness is to take fifteen pages to start my story, I should discard the first fifteen pages of everything I write.

Exercise

Take an inventory of your writing strengths and weaknesses. Not surprisingly, your strengths and weaknesses are often related. (As a martial artist, if my strength is in my punches, almost automatically my kicks must be a weakness.) Consider how you can use your strengths to understand and improve your weaknesses. For example, one of my strengths as a writer: a friendly, conversational style. Related weakness: a tendency to wander afield of the topic, just as I might in a long chat with a friend. Okay on the phone, not so great in writing. Understanding how the two are related helps me remember to look for and spot those places where I've wandered from a point, have used three too many examples, and have otherwise crept from being a friendly conversationalist to becoming a bore.

70
Accept hard challenges

Hard training sooner or later becomes a fact of every martial artist's life. Now and then the instructor will look at all the students lined up and decide to see if he can make them all puke before the session is over. Sometimes martial artists seek out hard training when they enroll in camps and seminars and try to learn as much as possible in a short period of time—staying on the mats and throwing people for hours on end.

Through these hard challenges, a martial artist develops endurance and self-confidence. He knows he can face tough challenges because he has already done so.

Writers also need to accept hard challenges. I've been asked to turn an article (complete with hard-won expert quotes) into a personal essay, throw out three chapters of a book and make a 3,000-word article into a 1,000-word article while adding more detail. I did these things although they were hard because the editor needed me to.

Linda Formichelli also describes, "I learned early on to write in a variety of styles, from light and fun kids' articles to obnoxious-bordering-on-dirty pieces for men. I've written on subjects ranging from how to peel a banana to the cats of wine country to artificial intelligence." Now that's hard training! The payoff? "When editors see that I have the ability to handle anything they can throw at me, I get more assignments," Linda says.

Exercise

The next time you have an idea for an article or short story or are offered an assignment but realize it will be hard to do for any one of a number of reasons (the difficulty of finding interview subjects, the departure from your usual style, the need for research in an area you're unfamiliar with) go ahead and write the piece or take the assignment. Consider it hard training to prepare you for a future writing career that will be full of the unexpected.

71

Obstacles are opportunities

In my particular style of martial arts, students are required to do board breaking during their promotion tests. The board breaking isn't all that important to the judges. What it mostly reveals is the student's willingness to persevere when the boards don't break. Board breaking is not difficult in the sense that if you perform the technique correctly, with power, the board will break. Boards don't put up a very stiff resistance to a determined blow. But they intimidate plenty of martial artists anyway. You know that if you slam into the board at an off angle, or if you slip while executing your technique, it's going to hurt when your precious body part bounces off the wood.

Through all the beginning and early intermediate belt levels, I broke my boards on the first try every single test. As I progressed through the ranks, the techniques used to break the boards grew more difficult, but I never had any problems breaking the boards. I never had to worry about persevering, at least not until I reached brown belt. And wouldn't you know, on my very first brown belt test, I had trouble breaking the boards. Now, in the whole scheme of the universe, this was not a very troubling problem. It bugged me, I admit, but I knew I was doing well enough on the other parts of the test to counterbalance this problem.

Then at my second brown belt test (this particular school required a total of six brown belt tests), the same thing happened. I couldn't break the boards at first—or even when I tried again. Finally I managed it, but I felt embarassed and not my usual competent and confident self. At the third test: same thing. I became upset. I was closing in on my black belt test, and I needed to be able to break boards for that. But I had developed some sort of mental block about the board breaking. I'd look at the boards, and they'd look back, and I'd lose the contest. Fourth test, again the same problem. Fifth test, still no boards breaking on the first or even second try. One more test to go and then I'd be eligible for black belt, and if I knew my instructor, I'd have to break twenty boards to promote to black belt. (I was right.)

Finally, on my sixth brown belt test, I arrived at the test with the determination that I was going to break every single board on the first try if I had to break my hands doing it. I was fiercely determined. And I did it.

I learned the degree of determination I needed to succeed at this. The obstacle gave me a chance to develop exactly the right type of mindset that I would need to survive my black belt test and other challenges that came along in my life.

For writers, obstacles also present opportunities. Rejections encourage us to rethink our ideas and reformulate them, perhaps coming up with an even better idea this time around. A limit on word count that will be hard to meet tests our writing skills and teaches us how to say the most with the fewest amount of words.

Instead of considering obstacles as insurmountable roadblocks in the way of your success, consider them opportunities to learn, to approach from a different angle, and to exercise your ingenuity and creativity.

Exercise

Learn to think of obstacles as "challenges." Instead of thinking, "This idiot editor wants me to chop a 3,000-word feature article into a 200-word sidebar by Tuesday? Clearly, she's tripping," which is hardly a positive spin, try, "This editor has challenged me to come up with a creative way to condense a lengthy story down to its essence." The first is a pain. The second might even be an interesting exercise.

72

Give your strongest effort with every try

Nothing irritates a martial arts instructor more than inconsistent effort. She doesn't care if you can't do the technique as long as you try your hardest with every single attempt. The only way a martial artist learns the skills necessary is by giving her strongest effort with every try. When she's doing a form, every block must seem like a real block, capable of deflecting a blow. Every punch must be targeted accurately and delivered with enough power to disable the attacker, even if the martial artist is just punching air. In other words, inconsistent effort leads to poor results, whereas giving one's best at all times creates a good martial artist.

As writers, it's sometimes tempting to give a good-enough effort to a client or editor, especially if you have a lot else going on and you know the good-enough effort will pass muster. But giving your strongest effort with each try is exactly what a professional does. If you can't give your best to an assignment, it would be better not to take it on. Remember, each of these efforts represent you. They go out into the world and stay out there. You don't want to be embarassed by them later. You always want to be able to say you did your best with every project.

Exercise

Don't take on rush jobs or allow clients or editors to pressure you into letting them see a "rough draft." No client or editor, no matter what they say, is really prepared for what a rough draft looks like. Trust me, I nearly derailed a book project once by letting the editor see a first draft of the project against my better judgment when she kept pestering me. (I still have nightmares in which I hear her gasp of horror as she reads that pitiful first draft.) I now have a policy of only allowing final, polished drafts out of my sight, and so should you.

Rush jobs are also fatal because you cannot do your best work under that type of pressure. Any good writing requires a few days to mature, a period where you leave it alone and do other tasks before coming back to it for a final edit. Create a policy that it takes you a week to do any writing project, even those that really take an hour to write. Even those quickies need their maturation time. Compromise this policy at your peril.

73

Never let fear create inaction

When martial artists begin training, they find a lot to fear. They fear not doing the techniques correctly. They fear falling down and getting hurt. They fear hitting someone else. They fear getting hit. To some degree, all of these fears are perfectly realistic: In martial arts training, you will fall down, you will hit other people, you will be hit, and some percentage of the time, all of the above will hurt.

But a martial artist has to learn to function despite those fears, without letting those fears stop her. The primary purpose of training is to learn to act despite fears. Pretty soon the fear goes away. A person can get hit, but it doesn't have to cause fear. A person can fall down and it doesn't have to cause fear. A person can even get hurt, and it doesn't have to cause fear. In fact, fear itself has no reality. It's a useful impulsive emotion to keep you out of too much trouble (i.e., so you'll stop sticking your hand in the fire) but that's all it is. You can't let it control your life.

For writers, fear creates inaction. They're afraid, so they don't do anything. They fear rejection. They fear criticism. They think if they put their work out there, something bad or negative could happen. And to some degree all of these fears are perfectly realistic. But that's completely beside the point.

Acknowledge that you have fears—of getting rejected, of being ignored—then act despite those fears. Fear may be a useful tool to keep you from sticking your hand in the fire, but it can be safely ignored in your writing career.

Exercise

Honestly ask yourself in what way is fear limiting you as a writer. Are you afraid of submitting your work for publication? Are you afraid of asking other writers their opinion of your work? Even if the results of your action are negative—your work gets rejected, other colleagues think your writing needs more polish—you can learn and grow from the experience. Fearfully letting the experience pass you by does not allow you to grow as a writer. Make it a goal to do one thing you fear as a writer each month, and learn what you can from it.

74
Nurture yourself

Beginning martial artists can be very hard on themselves. They see what others can do and feel inadequate or incompetent because they can't do those things—even if the person they're observing has been training for years longer than the beginner has, even if the person they're observing has been blessed with innate skills and talents few of us share. Even more advanced martial artists can be hard on themselves. They should have done better in that sparring match. They know how to counter that kick, so why didn't they? How come all the other brown belts seem to have no trouble memorizing *kata* (forms)?

But feeling inadequate and incompetent does not make you a good martial artist. Being hypercritical of yourself doesn't let you experiment, practice, grow and achieve. It freezes you and drains you. It can even lead to burnout.

As a writer, it's important for you to nurture yourself and your creativity, to be realistic about your craft but not overly negative. It's important to protect yourself from people who are unsupportive of your dreams and goals. And it's equally important to remember to congratulate and reward yourself when something good happens. As a beginner, it is a good thing when an editor says that although she'll have to pass on your idea, your query letter was very well-written. As a more advanced writer, it *is* a big deal when your article comes out in a major magazine, even if it's the fiftieth time you've placed an article. It *is* a big deal when you sign a book contract, even the third or fourth, and it calls for celebration. This is a hard, hard business, and marking these milestones helps you nurture yourself and feel good about your work.

Exercise

Give yourself a pat on the back when you accomplish something positive related to your writing. If you have finished an essay, treat yourself to a new novel you've been wanting to read (you can always check it out of the library). If a manuscript is accepted for publication, perhaps it's time to splurge on a piece of equipment that will make your writing life easier. At the minimum, sit back and give yourself props for a job well done. Or, steal this idea from one of my colleagues: exchange cards and small gifts with your writing buddy when one or the other of you has achieved something notable. (Decide ahead of time what counts as "notable.")

75
See the target beyond the target

A martial artist trains to go beyond the target—to see the target beyond the target. If he strikes *to* a target, seeing only the target in front of him, he's likely to stop his strike *at* the target. His strike doesn't go through the target, it stops on the surface of the target. This limits the amount of impact his blow generates. But if he thinks about striking *through* the target, if he visualizes his hand or foot plowing through the target and out the other side, he strikes a much more powerful, committed blow.

As writers, we also need to see the target beyond the target. This helps us commit to the work we're doing now because it's part of a larger picture, and it helps us plan a strategy for a writing career, instead of just hoping it will all work out.

For example, suppose you want to get published. That's your target. But what's the target beyond the target? *Why* do you want to get published? What happens next? If you never ask that question, you can never formulate an effective strategy to getting where you really want to go. If you want to get published just for the sake of getting published, it may be difficult to sustain the perseverance and hardheadedness you're going to need to accomplish the goal. But if you want to get published because it's the first step on the road to becoming a self-employed writer, no longer at the mercy of telecom industry layoffs, then it's easier to stay focused, because you have a greater strategy in mind. The individual setbacks won't deter you and make you stop. By knowing what you're trying to gain from each target—each goal—you're aiming for, you can strike a stronger, more committed blow.

Exercise

Formulate a "target beyond the target" for each of your writing goals. Doing so will help you see where you want to go, and it will help you envision alternatives and other approaches you can take to see your dreams come true.

For example, when I finished *Dojo Wisdom,* I wanted to do my part to publicize the book. I could have sent out press releases and e-mailed all my friends. Those are certainly publicity efforts. But by thinking beyond my target, which was to publicize my book, I focused on what I hoped to accomplish by publicizing my book. I hoped to sell copies of my book . . . I hoped to sell enough copies of my book so I could keep a roof over my head, and make the publisher want to publish my next book. Okay, that was better. That was a lot less vague than "I need to publicize my book." It gave me something concrete to focus on—selling copies of my book.

If a promotional possibility seemed likely to sell books, I'd do it. If it seemed like it wouldn't, I'd take a pass (having only so much time and energy to spend on promotional efforts). When I was offered a chance to host a weekly radio show on the Martial Arts Radio Network, I took the opportunity even though I wasn't paid for my time, because I knew I could talk about *Dojo Wisdom* and sell some copies of it. When I'm asked to talk to a reporter, I now try to find out if he or she is likely to mention my book in print. If so, I'm happy to do the interview. If not, the interview may not be worth my time. By understanding the target beyond the target, I'm able to make sensible decisions about how to spend my time and energy.

You can do the same.

76
Trust yourself

As martial artists train, they come to understand the damage they're capable of inflicting on others. They realize that they can kick someone and hurt him. They understand that they can throw someone and disable him. Or manipulate his joints and immobilize him. With this knowledge comes a responsibility to use the methods wisely and carefully. In the early stages of training, when martial artists recognize the possibility of hurting others, they do all sorts of things to prevent it. When working with partners, they move slowly instead of striking quickly like a snake. They spar from six feet away so that their kicks and punches don't actually touch their sparring partner. But it's difficult to learn to spar if you spar from six feet away. Eventually you have to move closer . . . eventually you have to learn to trust yourself. You have to trust that you have the skill, control and finesse not to hurt anyone in training.

Of course, it does happen that you still end up whacking a partner too hard (or vice versa) on occasion, and this'll make you feel bad, but then you rediscover that you do have control and finesse and you get back on track.

In other words, a martial artist takes an enormous step in his evolution when he learns to trust himself. When he knows what his body is capable of doing and knows that he has perfect control over it.

As a writer, you must also learn to trust yourself. This

means believing that you have the talent, aptitude and perseverance necessary to be successful as a writer. It means knowing that you will behave in a professional manner with editors and clients. It means realizing that you've finally polished that manuscript until it shines and there's nothing more you can do to make it better.

Developing self-confidence as a writer is a difficult thing. It needs to be balanced with a willingness to continue learning and improving. But if you always sell yourself short, it's difficult to make progress. Learn to trust yourself, to listen to yourself. Don't confuse being in a hurry to get a project done with being confident you've done the best that you could do. Distinguish between the two. Really attune yourself to the inner voice that says with satisfaction, "That's done!" and means that *that* is as good as it's possible to get.

Exercise

Learn to trust yourself by making a firm commitment to stop second-guessing yourself. Make a decision about your writing career (to send this query, dump that agent) by listening to your intuition and by using a clear, calm mind to arrive at the decision. Then, do not revisit the decision. You've made it using all available information, and it's done. Go on to the next thing. Over time, you'll develop trust in your ability to make wise decisions.

77

Act instead of hoping

People train in martial arts because they want to learn to act. They want to learn to defend themselves instead of hoping they never have to. They want to face their fears instead of pretending they don't exist. Martial artists train in the art of doing something rather than hoping things will work out okay. They want to know what to do if x happens. They want to know how to make y happen.

Writers also need to learn to act instead of hoping. It's not enough to hope your book sells well; you have to do everything you can to make it happen. It's not enough to hope the editor likes your article; you have to do everything you can to make it happen. International best-selling author Julia Cameron says, "All of my tools boil down to that Nike ad, 'Just do it.' Artists have to face many challenges, but I think there's a danger receiving too much sympathy and coddling from others when you really need to pick up a pen and just do it."

Writer Linda Formichelli puts it this way: "A lot of people say to me, 'I wish I could be a writer.' If I can do it, why can't they? The only difference between the writer and the wannabe is that the wannabe keeps on wishing and the writer gets off her duff, finds out what she has to do and does it." Linda goes so far as to say, "Hope keeps writers down. They send out an idea and say, 'I hope the magazine buys it.' Instead of just hoping, I take action to tilt things in my favor. I call experts to get the most compelling quotes for my query, and I find stats that show the editor that my idea is important to readers. I include my best clips. I follow up by phone or e-mail. In other words, I don't rely on fate to sell articles."

Exercise

Come up with ideas for how you can act in your writing career—right now, today. Remember, you have control over what you do. Instead of dashing off a query letter, popping it in the mail and hoping the editor likes it, waiting passively for the editor to make the next move, do your best to act. Take the time to do the research. Get the quote that will make your first sentence sizzle. Ask other writers for feedback to make your query as solid and convincing as possible. Then, knowing you've been thorough, send the query off. Don't forget to follow up with the editor in a few weeks. Then, in the meantime, go on to the next idea or project and act on it. Keep acting—keep knocking on doors—until one finally opens. The more action you take, the more likely you'll make progress in your career.

78
Limit unhealthy choices

After you've worked really hard for a couple of hours, throwing people over your shoulder, sparring the heavy bag, otherwise working up a good soaking sweat, the last thing you should do is take the exercise as permission to eat a quart of ice cream as soon as you get home. A martial artist knows that by limiting unhealthy choices, she becomes a better martial artist. If she eats right and commits to staying in shape, she can handle, physically, any challenges that come her way. She tends to remain healthier, able to look after herself and others. She's able to do her work.

She's careful about getting enough sleep. She knows that the occasional night on the town is fine, but every night on the town is not. She knows that drinking and drugging cloud her perception and awareness, and so she takes a pass. The more she thinks of herself as a martial artist—the more she thinks of herself as a warrior—the easier it is for her to make these kinds of healthy choices.

As a writer, you should also limit unhealthy choices. Of course getting or staying in shape and eating right contribute to a good long career, but beyond the physical, you must make healthy career choices.

Instead of doing only unpaid writing, which may be okay occasionally at the begining of your career, but which becomes an unhealthy choice after a while, pursue paying work as a writer. Instead of submitting only to contests and competitions (an okay choice that becomes unhealthy if it's all you do), submit to agents and editors.

Exercise

Ask yourself, "How does this choice benefit me?" While that may seem a cold, crass approach to decision-making, you can bet the people offering you the choice have thought long and hard about what they're going to get out of it.

As I've become more successful, I've been approached by friends and other writers I know who want to collaborate on books. At first, I said, "Yeah, that would be great," because I know and love these people, and because most of them have a little talent and I hated to disappoint them. They felt I knew how to write books and get them published and they wanted to be part of that—in other words, it would be a good choice for them.

One afternoon, when the fourth person in a month suggested we collaborate on a book, I found myself saying (to myself), "What on earth would be the point of that?" The book being proposed was one I could write perfectly well myself, it was in my niche, and why would I share all the proceeds with another writer when I'd be doing all the work? Writing the proposal, asking my agent to represent it, hammering out the editorial needs with the editor, doing the writing? I guess the other person thought supplying the idea was enough. But I've got plenty of ideas. I have a filing cabinet stuffed full of book ideas I'll never have time to write.

After this experience, I finally learned to say, "I can't do any projects without my agent's permission. If you want to write a book proposal, I can take a look at it and submit it to her for her thoughts." So far, the proposals have never been written. That's all I need to know. If someone was really serious about collaborating with me, they'd be willing to do some work.

As you become more successful, you will also be prevailed upon to help others get their foot in the door. It's fine to do this within reason. A brief critique of a query letter or a list of editors you work with can be done in an hour. That's a healthy choice. "Helping" a friend by writing an entire book takes months. That's an unhealthy choice.

79
You need a training partner

In the training hall, the people you practice the techniques with are called training partners or sparring partners. You can't learn martial arts without training partners. You'd be doing your techniques in front of a mirror and hoping they'd be effective in a street fight. But because you have these partners, you learn what it feels like to hit someone with a punch. You learn what it's like to have the punch deflected. Or how quickly you can find your feet swept out from under you. A good training partner challenges you and helps you become better. At the same time, you help your partner become better.

In the writing biz, writers often feel that other people—editors, agents, other writers—are opponents, people who are keeping you from getting what you want. But if you looked at it another way, you could see that these people are really your partners. You all want the same things—success in the writing business. If you can work with that editor to deliver exactly what she needs, then you're partners, not opponents. If you can listen to the agent's advice and develop a platform for your subject, then she will partner with you instead of turning you down flat.

And as for other writers . . . they can be your partners, too. Linda Formichelli says, "Some writers see other writers as their competition, and they jealously guard information from them. They'll never share information about a new market; they'll never give you one of their editors' names. But when these writers are facing a problem or a slow time, who will they turn to?" Well . . . no one.

Linda relates the story of an e-mail list she started with some friends so they could share leads. She found plenty of assignments through this shared list. But one writer didn't share: "He soaked up all the information but refused to give any himself. We eventually disbanded and then reformed the list without this guy. The miserly writer clearly felt that there wasn't enough work out there for all of us. He was wrong. There are thousands of magazines, and plenty of assignments to go around. Instead of thinking of other writers as opponents, I think of them as my partners in finding new work."

Exercise

In your next project, whether it's a book proposal, a query letter or a cold call to drum up business for your commercial copywriting, approach it from a new perspective. Think of yourself as being a partner to the gatekeepers (the agent, the editor). Don't think of them as your opponents that you have to outwit and get past somehow. If you consider your approach from this perspective, then instead of focusing on providing them what you want to provide, what you want to see in print, you'll be able to think about their needs and what they want from you. This change in perspective can mean the difference between getting published and remaining unpublished.

80

Learn from watching

Martial artists learn about their style through verbal instruction, physical practice and from watching others. They watch senior students do the techniques, they listen to the instructor describe the techniques, and they try to imitate what they've seen and heard. Imagine trying to learn any sport without being able to watch the participants—if you could only go by what you read in a book or what was told to you by a coach. You wouldn't do very well. You might think you were doing the techniques correctly, but you wouldn't have anything to compare it to. You would have no way of knowing if you were on track and if your techniques were accurate and effective. You would have no idea if you were even close.

Writers also need to learn from watching—watching other writers at work. And no, this doesn't mean going to their offices and sitting quietly while they pound away at the computer keyboard, although that wouldn't be a bad way to get an idea of what a writer's life is like.

Watching other writers means seeing what writers actually do as writers. What tasks do they perform in a given day? What is their time devoted to? Do they spend a lot of time hanging out in coffee bars talking about what writers do, or do they sit at their computers and write?

Learning from watching also means reading the work of other writers and mentally assessing whether yours measures up. It means being open to a really terrific turn of phrase and admiring it, not dismissing it. You don't want to slavishly imitate other writers, but their work can show you new ways to think about your own work, new ways to approach your own writing.

Track down a professional writer and interview him or her for a few minutes about the writing life. What does she spend her time on? What aspects did he not expect? As an aspiring writer, I was shocked to read an interview with a mystery author who talked about how she spent most of the day dealing with PR, promotion and administrative details and only got a chance to write late at night. I'd thought being a professional writer meant you'd have time to write! But when I became a professional writer, I found my days consumed with "business" with only nights and week-ends left for actual writing. Learning this early in your career can help you prepare for it. It can also help you understand the techniques that lead to success.

81

Understand what you observe

Martial artists focus—a bit obsessively, it's true—on observing the world around them, being aware of what's happening, and processing that information so that they can respond appropriately. Not only must they be aware of what's happening, but they have to understand what it means so they can act promptly and effectively.

Consider this: How many times have you heard kids shrieking in your neighborhood, and couldn't determine if they were laughing or crying? You had to get more information, right? You had to listen for a few more seconds, or walk outside to see what was happening. If you assumed the children were laughing, you might have been right—but you might have been wrong. If you assumed the children were screaming, and immediately dialed 9-1-1, you might have done the right thing, but you might have overreacted and had some explaining to do afterward—and you'd be reluctant to dial 9-1-1 again, even if you really should.

Writers also need to understand what they observe. Author Bob Spear says, "Pick it apart. Analyze it. Take a seat in a public place and listen to the dialogue between people. How do they talk? What do they talk about? Seek to understand their dialogue so you can recreate it later when you need it."

To build their writing careers, writers need to understand what they observe. In *Lesson #80: Learn from watching*, I talked about finding out what writers actually do with their time as writers. But watching alone doesn't reveal all the answers. You also have to understand what you're observing. In other words, you've established the fact that a certain writer functions in a certain way, but now you have to ask, *why* does the writer do it this way? That's where you understand what you're observing. Other important questions to ask in order to understand what you see include: Is it the most effective way possible? And is it the right way for you? Is it a technique you can use?

Take your interview from *Lesson #80,* and analyze it, particularly how it relates to you and your writing career. Don't jump to an immediate conclusion, but try to understand the writer's approach. Suppose the writer describes how he works four hours in the morning, knocks off for lunch and spends the rest of the day puttering around. You, being highly motivated, may automatically assume the writer could do better if he just worked harder. Personally, being a Type A, I'd probably jump to the same conclusion. But try to understand instead of judging. Ask why the writer does this. Is it really because the writer lacks motivation? Or is it because he knows that he can produce terrific prose that needs little editing or rewriting if he restricts himself to four hours of work a day? Perhaps he has found that working more hours is a waste of time because he just has to rewrite everything he produced in hours five through eight. Learning that, maybe *you* can try working a little less and still produce as much.

82

Sometimes, remain silent

Martial arts instructors restrict chatting during class. They expect students to remain quiet and to pay attention. Staying quiet helps keep the students focused on learning the techniques and concepts, not on the terrible thing their boss did today.

Often, students must save their questions until the

end of class. They focus on listening to the instructor and trying the techniques themselves. They don't burst out with every single question that pops into their heads. Frequently the instructor answers their questions by the time the training session has concluded, because she covers the material, or the student discovers the answer himself through practice. Saving the questions until the end prevents the waste of valuable training time. The instructor emphasizes *doing,* not talking about doing. So, early in their training, martial artists learn the value of silence in training.

They also learn the value of silence in de-escalating conflict. They learn not to respond to challenges or get into boasting contests with other people. They learn that remaining silent can defuse a tense atmosphere. If you keep your mouth shut, no one can misunderstand you.

Writers can use silence as an excellent tool in their work.

- If you focus on doing the writing, instead of talking about doing the writing, you'll make progress.
- Silence is an aid to awareness and observation.
- Silence can be an effective tactic when you interview people for your work. If you're trying to get a quote, instead of interrupting the interviewee to clarify your question, just let it be. If the interviewee answers with a simple "yes" or "no" and you need more than that, be silent for a moment. He or she may expand on the answer.
- Silence is also effective in negotiation. I once talked to an editor about writing a magazine ar-

ticle. She asked me point blank, "Does $1,500 sound right?" I was in the middle of chewing a cinnamon roll, so I couldn't answer "YES!!!!" immediately. The pause couldn't have lasted more than a second, when she rushed in and said, "Okay, how about $2,000?" Not bad for one second's work. "Umm, sure," I said, after nearly choking on the cinnamon roll. "That would be fine." Now I work a little silence into all my negotiations.

Exercise

Silence *is* golden. The next time you're asked to make a decision about your writing career—whether it's an editor calling with an offer or a client wanting a quote—allow a little silence into the conversation. Don't be so eager to say yes. Make sure you really want to do the project and that you'll be happy about the terms. I've never gotten into trouble stopping to think before I answer—and letting the silence do some work for me. But I have gotten into trouble rushing in and saying, "Absolutely, let's start tomorrow!"

83

Find your rhythm

When martial artists spar, their movements often resemble a dance. They act and react to each other in rhythmic ways. They get into a flow of attack and counter, defend and counter, playing off the techniques the other martial artist uses. When you're sparring in rhythm, it feels terrific. And it looks impressive to the people watching. You're attuned to your sparring partner, and you're demonstrating the beauty and control of good fighters.

Finding this rhythm takes practice. Beginners don't know how to spar each other. They do one technique and then stop. They don't counter what the other martial artist is doing. They just try to block it if they see it coming. But over time they develop a sense of rhythm, and they learn the dance, and they find it very satisfying.

As a writer, finding your rhythm or voice is equally satisfying. You won't use the same voice all the time, but you will probably use some variation of it. As a beginner, you may try out lots of different voices, searching for your own. I did the same. I used to go for an overwrought style. Then, in contrast, I tried for the simple Hemingway-esque approach. Later, because I was an academic, I developed a scholarly-type voice for my nonfiction work. None of these voices were bad but only when I developed confidence in my writing did I understand that my best writing was that which came most naturally—the writing that sounded as if I were talking to a friend.

My shameful secret? I can write in this style a lot easier than any other style. I just sit down, visualize a friend and start typing. My work requires some revision—the conversational approach tends to rely on passive voice and "to be" verbs—but the amount of revision required is much less than when I was still experimenting and had not found my natural rhythm.

Find your rhythm. For most people, a simple, natural style works wonders. If you have to rewrite and revise each piece nineteen times, you're trying too hard and it probably shows in your writing. Don't assume that fiction has to be more literary than nonfiction. Use your natural voice—just try it—and see if it isn't easier and more pleasurable to write (and ultimately more successful).

84

Practice broken rhythm training

When a martial artist performs a form, she wants to establish a rhythm of flowing smoothly from one technique to another. That shows her grace, agility and balance. When a martial artist spars, she often establishes this rhythm, too, especially when she knows her sparring partner well. She does a roundhouse kick, her partner counters with a reverse kick, she blocks the reverse kick and counters with a punch. Often, we seek this rhythm as martial artists. It builds our strength, clears our minds, refines our timing skills.

But rhythm can also be detrimental to our success. If I get into a rhythm too often when I spar, my opponent can begin to anticipate what techniques I will use and when. This knowledge can tell him to nail me with a front kick the next time I come charging in with my reverse punch. Sometimes I have to break my rhythm. To do this, I practice broken rhythm training. I don't allow one technique to flow smoothly from the next. I do the unexpected. If I always follow up a reverse punch with a crescent kick, I stop doing that. If I never use roundhouse kicks to the head, I start. If I always lead with my left foot, I start leading with my right. All of this breaks up the rhythm, teaches me how to use more techniques differently, and ensures that my sparring partners won't be able to guess what I'm going to do next.

A writer often seeks to find the flow—the rhythm where the words come, and they're good, and the characters do what they're supposed to be doing, and good heavens, writing *is* a lot more fun than bleeding. But sometimes this flow leads us right into a blind alley. We look up, bleary-eyed, and see that we've totally abandoned the plot, and how the hell are we going to get our heroine out of the brothel? Or we see that our thousand-word article on nutritional supplements has turned into a ten-page screed on the iniquities of the beauty industry.

We have to be willing to break up the rhythm. If it means going back to the beginning and rewriting the whole manuscript so that the heroine doesn't end up in the brothel in the first place, then that's what needs to be done. If it means scraping the whole screed—or at least setting it aside for a different use—then that's what needs to be done. That's broken rhythm training. It's hard and it takes discipline. But it's necessary. Sometimes, in flow, we write something so heartbreakingly beautiful, we're convinced we have found some part of the Truth. But if it's smack in the middle of page sixty of a lighthearted murder mystery, it's going to have to come out.

Being in rhythm, in flow, is a transcendental feeling. We like it. Broken rhythm training, by contrast, is more conscious, more deliberate, and a whole lot less fun. But it can mean the difference between success and failure.

Exercise

Practice broken rhythm training in your writing. The next time you're in flow, stop in the middle of a sentence before you're totally exhausted. Put the piece aside. Interrupt the flow. Hard, isn't it? But useful. Now, when you go back to the piece, you can look at it realistically. Were your words as beautiful as you thought? Is the piece headed in the right direction, or did you let the rhythm take over? Even better, when you go back to the piece, you can simply complete the sentence you interrupted and you're ready to get going again. That saves a lot of anguish and time staring at the computer screen wondering what you should say next.

85

Explore other styles

Martial artists constantly seek ways to become more effective fighters. If they now study a style that focuses on striking, they may later explore a grappling style. If they study a style from a Korean tradition, next they'll look at one from a Chinese tradition. By exploring other styles, the martial artist builds his arsenal and becomes a more effective fighter. But he doesn't necessarily abandon the techniques that have already proven useful to him. He simply adds the new ones to his catalog.

For writers who have found their style, their voice, the idea of exploring other styles excites them enough to provoke a yawn. They did that as beginners, thank you very much, but now they've finally found their voice, and it works, and they're sticking with it. But exploring other styles, other voices, isn't about abandoning the one that works for you. It just means finding variations on your usual voice. (A martial artists doesn't abandon martial arts in order to learn basket-weaving. He just tries another type of martial art.)

A simple variation might be to use a different point of view than you normally do. If you always write in the first person, try the third. Or try an unreliable narrator. (Think how much fun that could be!) Try to write from the opposite gender's perspective. Write for a children's audience. None of these approaches is a complete break from your normal rhythm, just a variation. The variations keep you and your writing from becoming stale and predictable. They enlarge your arsenal of techniques.

Exercise

Unearth an old manuscript that you never felt quite satisfied with. Re-envision it using a variation of your normal voice. If you told the story from one character's perspective, try telling it from another. Or tell the backstory instead of the story you have. (How did these characters get here after all?) Try an omniscient narrator. Write it from the point of view of the dog. In other words, apply broken rhythm training to the manuscript as an experiment. You may still be dissatisfied with the result, but the experience may have inspired you to solve a problem you're having in your current story. Or maybe it just gives you a chance to flex some writing muscles.

86

Take what you can use, discard the rest

Bruce Lee taught his students to devote time to learning a specific martial arts style, and then to explore other styles at will, taking what they could use—what worked for them—and discarding the rest. He meant that once you had a basic understanding of a martial arts style, no matter what it was—Karate or Kung Fu, Tae Kwon Do or Jujitsu—you could add to it from other styles, take away what didn't work and essentially develop your own personal martial art.

Most martial artists understand the sense in that. They see that any one style, no matter what, has certain limitations. The grappling styles don't strike. The striking styles don't grapple. Kung Fu doesn't use high kicks. Tae Kwon Do doesn't use many hand techniques. But by fusing various parts of different styles together, the martial artist can learn what to do in any situation. But he has to be willing to discard the rest.

For example, I have been taught Hapkido techniques that simply do not work for me when I try them on a taller opponent. Since most people are taller than I am, these techniques don't ever go into my arsenal. On the other hand, I have learned some nice joint locks from Hapkido that they never taught me in Tae Kwon Do, and those I kept.

In writing, you face a dizzying array of choices. Not only can you write in a thousand different ways for a thousand different markets, but you can also pursue a gazillion allied opportunites—to be a paid speaker, to freelance as an editor or reviewer, to publish your own work. All of these may be good opportunities, but you must pick and choose the best.

I happen to make a good living writing books. This is a bizarre fluke in the publishing industry, so don't tell anyone. (I'm always waiting for someone to find out and put a stop to it.) Because so few writers actually make a living writing books, for a long time, I kept thinking I needed to do something different, like commercial writing, or editing, or PR work.

But it finally dawned on me that until I stop making a good living writing books, maybe I should discard the rest. Other opportunities will still exist if publishers stop acquiring my books. And just think, if I focus on writing and promoting my books, instead of wasting time and energy chasing other opportunities, I'll probably keep making a living writing books.

Keep in mind that this is just me. I'm the kind of person who goes to the cafeteria, finds the food she likes best and puts a lot of one thing on her plate (usually potatoes). Author Bob Spear is a different kind of writer. He owns a bookstore, he runs a book review service, he freelances as an editor and he writes and self-publishes books. This would make me put my head down and howl, but Bob relishes it. So it's not about what I would do, or what Bob would do, but what works for you.

Remember to pick what works for you and discard the rest. If you find yourself having success in a particular niche, don't fight it. Choose it if it works for you. Don't feel you must do everything other writers do. Maybe you like having a regular full-time job and writing on the side. You don't have to become a full-time free-lancer, if what you have works for you.

87
Finish the fight

Martial artists are taught to finish the fight. They learn not to rely on one "killer" blow to do the job. They know they may have to perform a series of techniques to stop an attack. They don't do one kick and then stop, confident they've dealt a disabling blow. They keep on doing techniques until they've won the fight.

The phrase "finish the fight" also prepares them mentally to do what needs to be done and to never give up. In other words, if they're not prepared to finish the fight—force the attacker to flee, disable or disarm the attacker, or otherwise end the fight—then they should not get in the fight in the first place.

Writers can take a lesson from this. Only if you're willing to go the distance does it make sense to get started. Otherwise, you're better off spending your time, money and energy on something else with greater chances of rewards. Pursuing a writing career and achieving success as a writer is going to be even harder than you imagine, no matter how hard you think it's going to be. So if you're going to give up at any time before you finish the fight, don't bother getting in the ring.

This is not meant to discourage aspiring writers. It's meant to help you understand the attitude you have to have to succeed. You have to commit to finishing the fight, you have to be willing to do whatever it takes to succeed, no matter how long it takes and no matter how tough the road. If you have or can develop this mindset, then you will win—you will finish the fight.

Exercise

Examine your purpose as a writer. Do you enjoy writing for your own pleasure? That's fine, and it's certainly a legitimate hobby. Some people can tomatoes; some people write stories. But if you're eager to see your words in print and want to be a published, successful author, you have to be prepared to fight hard for the opportunity. If you're not prepared, then keep your writing as a rejuvenating hobby, something you enjoy doing, and don't feel that you must somehow gain legitimacy by getting published if you're really not prepared for or interested in the fight.

88
Smile when you spar

Sparring is a form of mock combat in which you pair up with a partner and trade controlled kicks and punches to practice your techniques. In general, you don't go full power (that's a good way to put your training partner in the hospital). Sparring has rules and regulations, such as you can't kick below the belt, or you can't strike to the kidneys, depending on the style. These guidelines prevent you from harming your partner (and vice versa). Sparring is not intended to simulate a street fight. It's just about learning to take a hit, learning how to use techniques in combination, learning how not to flinch when you see a punch headed your way. In a real street fight, you'd certainly kick below the belt, and you'd do your best to ram your attacker's head into the brick wall behind you. But sparring isn't like that. You may be very serious about the drills, and about seeing the openings and about scoring the points, but it's not an actual fight. It's not actual self-defense. It's sparring.

And sparring is a lot of fun. My instructor used to say, "Aren't you having fun?" and I'd say "Yes, sir," because I was, and then he'd say, "Then you should smile when you spar." So I did, and for a long time I thought by smiling I was sharing my enthusiasm for sparring. Until one day after a match, my partner walked away and muttered to one of his friends, "Jeez, I hate it when she smiles! It's so evil!"

Which just means that anything is open to misinterpretation, even a friendly smile.

But really, the reason I smile when I spar is because I know this isn't a street fight, and I know it's a lot of fun. It relaxes me to smile and I'm more effective when I'm relaxed.

Writers sometimes need to be reminded to smile when they spar. You may need to remember that it isn't as deadly serious as all that. That in the whole scheme of things, one rejection letter means nothing and it's certainly not worth ruining a day over. Sometimes you need to remember that you got started as a writer because you find writing fun. You love to write, you love to create. You lose yourself putting the words on the page. The act of writing, like the act of sparring, is fun—or should be fun. So don't rob yourself of the joy of writing just because the business of writing can be competitive and awful. Smile when you write. Worry about the rest when you're done writing.

Exercise

Separate the business of writing from the act of writing. Otherwise, it's easy to drain the joy out of it. The business of writing—the rejection letters, the demands for rewrites, the late checks, the pay-on-publication woes—all of that is the serious, gotta-make-a-living part that can be frustrating, nerve-wracking and ulcer-inducing. But the business of writing is not the act of writing. The business of writing needs attention, but it shouldn't get all of your attention. Give yourself permission to hate the business of writing if you must, but don't let that dislike spoil the act of writing. Maybe dealing with that pile of rejection letters makes your blood boil, but you should smile when you write.

89
Use the right equipment

Each martial arts style requires different equipment. A Tae Kwon Do class requires a uniform and protective gear for sparring. A Kendo class requires a wooden sword (a bokken) and special body armor. The protective gear you use in Tae Kwon Do is not appropriate for use in Kendo. (In Tae Kwon Do, no one's smacking you with a wooden sword.) In Karate, you might invest in a bo and nunchaku, equipment (weapons) that you would never use in a T'ai Chi class. The uniform you wear to a Kung Fu class would be out of place at the Jeet Kune Do school where everyone wears casual workout clothes.

A martial arts *dojo* (training hall) will be appropriately equipped for the training. You wouldn't want to attend a Judo class without tatami (mats) on the floor. And in Judo you might not need kicking targets, but in Tae Kwon Do, you do.

In other words, to be an effective martial artist, you have to have the right equipment.

To be an effective writer, you have to have the right equipment as well. You need to devote resources to your writing career just as you would to any business, even if you don't see an immediate return on your investment. So invest in and use the right equipment.

Exercise

Equip yourself as a professional. This does not mean going out and spending $10,000 on a state-of-the-art office suite with enough technology to make the entire Silicon Valley drool. It means investing in the equipment you'll need to be an effective writer. You know that you have to use a computer, have e-mail and Internet access, and be available by phone. Even if you don't have a penny to your name, you need to find and use this equipment. Make a plan.

If you can't buy a computer right away, consider leasing one. Use the computers at the public library. Many cities have Internet cafes where you can access your e-mail for a nominal fee. If you don't have the $30 a month for Internet access, or you don't have a computer, this can be a reasonable temporary measure.

Consider bartering your writing services for equipment you might need. Let friends and family members know that you've started a writing career and let them know what equipment you need. Many people have old computers sitting in their basements, and they'd love to do a good deed and give the computer to you.

Invest in the equipment you need. When enough editors started asking for my fax number, I stopped giving the number of the copy center (which would accept faxes on my behalf for $1 a page) and bought a fax machine. When editors started asking for my e-mail address, I got online. More recently, when readers started asking for my website, I hired a webdesigner. Remember, investing in your equipment makes you effective as a professional.

90
Imagination is a weapon

Although martial artists train in the use of physical techniques to stop an attack, they learn that they can often avoid having to use physical strikes at all if they just use their brains. In other words, if they walk away from the fight, they won't have to hit anyone.

Martial artists and self-defense instructors delight in telling stories about how they or their students or people they know got away from an attacker without ever hitting him. Sometimes the defender just yelled. Sometimes she used a clever ruse to get away. Sometimes she faked a faint, and sometimes she pretended that her big nasty boyfriend was on the way. The possibilities are endless. But the underlying theme is that martial artists learn to rely on their imaginations to get out of potentially violent situations. They learn that their imaginations can be extremely powerful weapons.

For writers, imagination is also a powerful weapon, and not just in the sense of using your imagination to create a powerful piece of writing. Your imagination can give you creative ideas for becoming a successful writer. Instead of doing exactly what everyone else does, you could try a different, creative approach and perhaps be more effective.

For example, you know that everyone wants to write the big feature stories in the national consumer magazines, including the magazines' staffers. Instead of following the traditional route and querying for one of those big features, use your imagination. What else does a magazine editor need written? She needs those roundup articles at the front of the magazine ("5 Must-Haves for the Beach!"). You can imagine that not very many writers propose those articles, and you can also imagine that the staff writers have probably written some variation of "5 Must-Haves for the Beach!" more times than they can count and if they have to do it one more time, they'll scream. But you might even enjoy writing the article and it will give you a foot in the door at the magazine.

Exercise

Give your imagination a workout. Instead of pursuing only traditional avenues, see what else you can do to get where you want to go. For example, suppose you have a great idea for a book, but you get the thumbs-down because no one thinks you can market it. Your first response might be to insist you can, and your second might be to trash the whole idea, but your third idea might be to market the book . . . before you've written the book. In other words, become the expert on the subject, get interviewed on radio, write articles about it, join organizations associated with it and then once you've shown you can do your stuff, try to find a publisher again. They'll listen this time—and if they don't, you'll have already created a market that you can exploit, so maybe you can use your imagination and self-publish.

Not long ago, I had an idea for writing a book about selling your writing. Most books on this topic focus on commercial writing, but my theory was that most people don't care to do that kind of writing. They want to write books and magazine articles, and they want to learn how to make a living at it. So I got together a bunch of people who make a good living writing articles and books and put together a proposal that almost, but not quite, made it onto a publisher's list. Unfortunately, some competing titles were coming out, so it was no go. I really liked the idea but stuck it in a drawer. At the same time, I was getting more and more requests from writers who wanted to know about the writing business. I was giving lots of writing workshops and spending a lot of time communicating with individual writers. In fact, I was spending too much communicating with individual writers, to the detriment of my work. So I began thinking about putting together an e-course for writers. But I didn't have time to develop the course . . . until using my imagination, it occurred to me that the book proposal, in which I had already invested a lot of time and energy, could become the basis for this e-course. Two problems solved at once, and instead of moldering in a drawer, my proposal turned into a course instead of a book.

So remember, your imagination is a weapon!

91
When you enter the *dojo*, abandon your worries

When the martial artist walks into the *dojo* (training hall), she needs to focus on her training. She needs to think about doing her techniques as perfectly as possible and learning as much as she can during this training period. If she's distracted, her training won't go well. If she's focused on what happened at work, she can actually endanger herself, because she won't be paying attention to the kicks flying her way. Martial artists quickly develop the ability to shed their worries at the door. (Don't worry, they can pick them up again later.) One of the consequences is that training becomes a way to relieve the martial artist of burdens, to help her de-stress, to aid her in keeping her life balanced and her troubles in perspective. What seemed to be a big problem when she walked into the training hall can seem much more manageable when she walks out, once she's had a chance to stop thinking about it for a while.

When a writer sits down to write, she needs to do the same thing. She needs to abandon her worries. She needs to not feel guilty about her kids, or about the laundry not getting folded. She also needs to abandon her worries about her writing. She needs not to obsess over whether she really has any talent or if she'll ever get published. As yoga teacher and writer Debz Buller puts it, "Make your space sacred. Do not let the outside world intrude upon the energy of what you do in this space. Like putting on your uniform or your wraps in preparation for sparring practice, keeping your writing space sacred only for this use will allow for creative flow and comfort in producing that flow and productivity."

Exercise

Create a space only for your writing. You don't need to go so far as to have a ritual when you enter it, although you can say, "I'm abandoning all my worries as I enter here." Personally, I'm all for rituals if they help you do what needs to be done.

This space should be set aside and reserved for your writing. Your spouse isn't allowed to pry, your kids aren't allowed to borrow the paper you have stashed there. It's just for you. The space doesn't have to be an office, although it can be. I now have an office where I do my paying writing, and I have a little corner in the living room where I do my fun writing. (The two are not mutually exclusive, but you can understand why I use separate spaces for each task.) A long time ago I found a wonderful wooden chest about the size of one drawer of a filing cabinet with a shiny brass lock on it. For years I have kept my novel-in-progress tucked in there, safe from prying eyes but readily accessible. Try to find a similar safe space for your work. When you enter the space, or pick up your work, don't let anything else intrude.

92

Your power improves every day

No martial artist is at the peak of her skill when she first walks into the training hall. (Thank goodness.) She knows that as she practices and learns more about the techniques, her power will grow. As she gains strength and fitness, she becomes a stronger martial artist. She sees the progress she makes as she goes through the ranks. What was difficult a few months ago is no longer so difficult. In fact, it's easy. What seemed impossible to memorize a few weeks ago is now second nature. The martial artist realizes that as long as she keeps training, her power will keep growing.

Your writing power grows every day, too—as long as you're writing. When I was a younger writer, I used to hope desperately that this was the day or the month when I would finally master the craft, that my writing would finally be so good that no one could turn it down. One day, I realized that it would be a shame if this was as good as it got. Wouldn't it be too bad if my skills were frozen at a certain level, and I could never improve them? Even though I've been publishing for years, my skills improve with each book. My style becomes more accessible. My examples more concrete. My turns of phrase fresher. It's exciting to think I can get better every day if I just keep working at it.

So don't be discouraged if you feel you have a long way to go to master the craft, or if you're still grappling with grammar issues. (One of my favorite authors, who shall remain nameless, apparently cannot write a single page without at least six run-on sentences. I always wonder if her editors are out to lunch or if they just don't dare point this out to a writer of her stature. But she's still a fabulous storyteller, and the run-ons, it could be argued, are merely stylistic.) Be encouraged by the fact that your powers grow every day, as long as you keep writing. Eventually, the grammar stuff will make sense (I hesitate to admit this but I was in graduate school before it all fell into place for me), your style will work itself out, you'll find your voice, and it will be beautiful. And then you'll get even better than that.

Exercise

Every few months, make a point of going over work you've done in the past (at least a year or so ago) to see how your powers have grown stronger. This exercise still makes me cringe. (I don't even like to read my books after they come out, because I know I've moved on since the manuscript was written.) But I do it anyway. I think it's good for me to remember that I still haven't conquered the passive sentence structure tendency. I don't want to get too complacent about that—I still need to be vigilant. And every now and then I'll read something of mine that makes me go, "Dang! I'm a gooooooood writer." And that's a nice feeling, too.

93
Your voice is powerful

Martial artists learn to *kihop* or *kiai* (the martial arts shout) to concentrate their energy and focus on a target or a goal. They use the shout to summon their Chi. They also use it to scare off the bad guys. The actual words don't matter as much as the shout does, because the shout draws attention to the attacker, which is the last thing he wants. It makes it clear to the attacker that you're not going to be an easy victim to mess with. And it tells the attacker, in no uncertain terms, that what he's about to do is not okay, in case he wasn't clear about that.

So martial artists recognize that their voices are powerful weapons.

As a writer, your voice is powerful, too. Sometimes, though, we feel our voices are lost in the cacaphony of all the other voices out there also clamoring for attention. But it's important to remember that your voice is powerful even if the environment around you is noisy.

The key is to find your distinctive voice, the one that is characteristically you. Martial artists can distinguish the shouts they hear—they know which of their colleagues and students are yelling, even if they're not in the same room—

and that's how you, too, can break through the noise. You cultivate your distinctive voice, knowing how powerful it is. This is not to say that you should have an artificial style—a shriek or high-pitched whine may get a bit of attention, but it's not as effective as your natural voice shouting.

Exercise

Remember your voice is powerful. It's easy to forget this and lose sight of it when thousands of other writing voices out there compete for attention. But start small. Seek to be heard by a local group of people, a magazine with a small readership. Build from there. As your writing success grow, your voice will become more powerful. Count on it.

94

Accept differences

Martial artists learn that some techniques, tools and strategies are effective for them, and others are not. Martial arts instructors understand that not all of their students will find the same techniques and strategies effective. They also know that not everyone will find martial arts as empowering as they'd wish. In other words, not everyone achieves a black belt because not everyone wants to.

And that's okay. Being a black belt is a good thing for me, and it means a lot to me. It has a certain currency among other martial artists. And I think other people might be missing out on something if they never give martial arts a try. But I don't think everyone should be a black belt. And I don't think people are total losers if they're not.

As a writer, accepting differences helps you grow and learn. You will find that some people like what you write and some people don't. That's okay. They're entitled to their opinions. Rejoice about the one and don't lose sleep over the other. Accept that people have different interests, wants and needs, and don't take it personally. There's nothing wrong with you if a reader doesn't like mysteries and that's what you write. And there's nothing wrong with you if it's just your particular mysteries the reader doesn't like (nothing wrong with the reader, either). It just is. Accept it. Move along.

Consider the editor who rejects your brilliant article idea. It's like the martial artist who doesn't use jumping kicks. She doesn't find them effective for her. It doesn't mean jumping kicks are stupid. It doesn't mean the martial artist is stupid. It just means that particular martial artist doesn't find that particular technique effective for her. At some other time or place, the martial artist might. Just not right now. In other words, no need to judge the kick or the martial artist. Maybe you can convince the martial artist (editor) to try the kick (article) but maybe not. And it doesn't have a whole lot to do with you.

Exercise

Cultivate an attitude of acceptance. Accept that sometimes your work will be right on target for an editor or reader and sometimes it won't. Realize that it doesn't always have anything to do with you or your writing. Learn what you can from the experience and keep moving forward.

95

Never reveal your strategy

Unless a martial artist is trying to teach a student, he doesn't announce his strategy to his partners or opponents. He doesn't say, "I'm going to use feints to draw your guard and make you commit to a kick, then counter from your kick." This would be a good way to lose the match. In the same way, he doesn't telegraph his moves (or at least, he tries not to). Any number of subtle signals can "tell" his opponent that he's about to do a certain technique. For example, if the martial artist suddenly leans back, shifting his weight to his back leg, the opponent can guess that he's going to do a kick with his front leg. Experienced fighters can recognize subtle shifts of body position and can anticipate the strikes that will follow.

So a martial artist tries not to telegraph his kicks. He tries not to signal his intention or announce his strategy. He's trying to win the match or score points on his opponent. He needs to keep his game plan to himself.

Writers often reveal their strategy too early in their writing. They give away the plot in the first three pages, they telegraph the villain's "amazing" transformation to hero three hundred pages ahead of time, that type of thing. The result? Their work comes across as predictable. "I knew that was going to happen" isn't necessarily a compliment. Of course, we can understand the importance of this in plotting the novel, but what about other aspects of the writer's life? What's to reveal? Doesn't everyone go about getting published in much the same way? What's wrong with letting everyone know your marketing plan? Isn't the idea to get some publicity?

Yes and no. Of course you should discuss your work and your plans with trusted advisors—friends who support you, your agent, your editor. But often it's not to your benefit to describe it to other people, particularly non-writers who don't know much about the business. This can put you on the defensive as they wonder why you're not successful sooner or how come you're not getting a six-figure advance like all the other writers they hear about.

Exercise

Keep certain aspects of your writing life and strategy private. If you've finally gotten the courage up to start submitting article ideas to editors, for example, you don't have to tell anyone except maybe a friend or your writing group who'll support you. The last thing you need is your neighbor asking you every single day, "So has your article been published yet?" If your idea receives only rejections, now you have to explain this to everyone. "No one wanted your idea?" they'll say (having no clue what the competition is like). The implication being that you're a total loser. Well, *you* know it takes perseverance and fortitude and you'll keep trying, but they may not know, no matter how you try to tell them. It's discouraging. You just know they're saying to their friends, "You know Joe? He's trying to be a writer. Poor slob, *no one* wants his ideas." Argh. You don't need that in your life. Instead, wait until you've got the contract in your pocket, then casually mention you have an article coming out in next week's *Time* magazine.

96

Don't allow your opponent to control the match

The person who controls the match—the tempo and timing—will likely win the match unless the other fighter gets lucky. An effective fighter knows that if she's forced on the defensive, she'll have fewer opportunities to win the match. She'll spend her time warding off blows and won't be able to score points on the opponent. Instead of hoping to get lucky, she acts to keep her opponent from controlling the match. She tries to take control by being more aggressive, feinting, drawing the other fighter out. She doesn't let herself get pushed into a position where all she can do is counter the other fighter's kicks.

Writers, who are up against what can seem like a big opponent (competition in the marketplace), sometimes let the opponent control the match. They feel there's not much more that they can do than send out query letters when they have a good idea. If these don't slip through the editor's guard, then they think they've lost the match. The marketplace has all the control. That's what many writers think, anyway.

But the truth is, you have more control than that. You can control how you act and how you feel about what happens in your career. You can control the number of queries you send out. (The number of queries sent is proportionate to the number of acceptances you get. In other words, zero queries equals zero acceptances; whereas 1,000 queries will, I promise, get at least some result.)

As Bob Spear says, "The writers' marketplace can be brutal. If what you're writing isn't being accepted, try to find out why. Improve, and if you still aren't getting accepted, think about self-publishing. Many who have self-published have proved their worth and eventually got picked up by the mainstream."

Exercise

You can take control of your writing career. Consider the various ways in which you've given up control to the other "side." Have lots of rejections convinced you to stop sending out queries? Take a query workshop at a writer's conference and send more. Have poor sales made editors wary of taking on your next book? Get those book sales up any way you can. You can't control everything that happens, but you can take charge of your career.

97
Practice your kicks 10,000 times

A martial arts master once told me, "You have to practice a kick at least 10,000 times before you start to understand it." Now, if he had told me that on my first day of class, I would probably have been a little discouraged, but I wasn't a beginner when he told me this, and I conceded that he was right. It coincided with my experience. Even if, as a beginner, I could do the kick without falling over after the first ten tries or so, I really didn't have any idea what the kick was about, I didn't have any clue about technique until I had done it 10,000 times. And that 10,000 times was only the beginning. At that point—after 10,000 tries—I was only scratching the surface.

So if you have to practice your kicks 10,000 times before you start to understand them . . . then as a writer you have to practice your craft at least the same amount. In writing, there really is no substitute for experience. You may have an ear, you may have talent, but in the end a writer becomes a writer simply by writing a lot. The good news is, the sooner you get started, the sooner you're on your way to understanding the craft.

When a certain level of competency has been achieved—and it will come sooner than you think if you keep at it—then you will write as if it were second nature. It will simply be a reflex that happens automatically. That doesn't mean you can stop developing and growing, it just means you won't have to focus so much on process. You will be confident that this time, just like last time and next time, you'll be able to produce a good piece of writing. Achieving that confidence and that competence is worth the time it takes to get there.

Exercise

Have you done your 10,000 kicks today? If you're having trouble getting your daily writing in, try a different approach. Compose into a tape recorder while you're on a walk. Treat yourself to coffee and a scone at Starbucks while you write. No one says you have to do the writing the same way in the same place, so long as you do it.

98

The Master respects his profession

A martial artist respects what he does. He does not apologize for being a master of the warrior arts. If he didn't believe in the martial arts, he would not be a master. Because he respects his profession, he tries to be a good role model. He tries to set a good example and to show others how to respect the profession as well. If he has students or potential students who do not show proper respect for what they are learning, he dismisses them. He takes what he does seriously. He believes it is important.

A writer must also respect his profession. Too often, we downplay or even denigrate what we do. "Well, it's not brain surgery," we'll say. And that's true. But that doesn't mean it lacks value. Being a good writer is at least as valuable as being a good plumber, and we know how important plumbers are.

One of the ways you can show respect for your profession is to treat it like a profession. Nora Roberts, who publishes four or five best-selling novels each year, reports that she writes in her office from nine-to-five every day, just like any other person with a job. She believes that her writing is a business and she has to treat it like a business. So just because she's had a string of best-sellers, she doesn't kick back and drink daiquiries under the palm trees. She respects her profession and treats it seriously.

When I agree to coach new writers, I always ask a series of questions designed to find out if they're serious enough about the profession. If they're not, I don't want to waste my time (or theirs). I expect coaching clients to be professional and business-like and to commit to learning the writing business as well as the writing craft.

Exercise

Get into the habit of treating your profession with respect. Be as professional as you can about your writing. Don't let yourself get into the habit of saying things like, "Well, it's better than a real job." And don't fall into the trap of thinking one type of writing is "better" than another. If you write commerical copy, good for you. If you write potboilers, there's nothing to be ashamed of. Be proud of what you do.

99
Adventure feeds the spirit

You can't become a martial artist without some sense of adventure. Otherwise you'd stick with something safe and sane like basketball or football. As martial artists learn their skills and techniques, they discover that a bit of adventure helps them become better martial artists. If they've never attended a tournament before, they'll give it a try. They'll attend a training camp or seminar for the fun of it. They'll embark on new challenges because this keeps their enthusiasm for training fresh.

Adventure is important for writers, as well. All too often, we spend so much time behind our computers that we forget there's a whole world out there waiting for us to explore it. If you feel isolated and bored, chances are you'll lose enthusiasm for your writing. So a little adventure—getting out from behind the monitor—can make a world of difference. My particular adventure—starting Tae Kwon Do lessons—got me out of the house, introduced me to people I'd never otherwise have met in professions I didn't know anything about. It opened up a whole new career for me. Other writers have gone to graduate school or lived in other countries for six months. One writer spent time in an ashram seeking a spiritual adventure.

Exercise

Go on an adventure. It doesn't have to be costly or time-consuming, it just has to be different from what you normally do. If you haven't been to the zoo in fifteen years, now's the time. If you've always wanted to go to L.A. but never found the time, find the time. You can even visit your own hometown as if you were a tourist, stopping at all the sites you never see because you live there. Feed your spirit and your writing will wake up.

100
Create

A martial artist trains. He uses his martial arts every day, even when he's old or disabled or getting a bit forgetful. He arranges his life to accommodate for being a martial artist.

A writer creates. She writes every day, even when she's old or disabled or getting a bit forgetful. She arranges her life to accomodate for being a writer.

It doesn't matter if she wins awards or the acclamation of her peers or financial success or any of the accoutrements of fame. What matters is, she creates. She doesn't wait for the muse to arrive, or for the time to be perfect. She writes, now.

Exercise

You know what this exercise is going to be: Put down this book and go write. Right now.

Conclusion

When I started on the journey—the journey of becoming a martial artist and the twin journey of becoming a writer—I didn't know what was in store for me. In fact, just the other day, I said to a friend, "Do you know, nothing in my life has actually gone according to plan?" What I meant is that nothing in my life goes according to *my* plan. It does, however, go exactly according to the universe's plan, which I could make good money from if only I could guess it ahead of time.

You don't know what your writing journey has in store for you. Some of you are farther along the Way than others and might be able to make a good guess. But no matter where you are, there's still the journey left up ahead. I don't know where it will lead me. I'm keeping my fingers crossed that it'll be a good destination, and not more of those Learning Experiences that I've had a few too many of in my life. But if what's in store for me is a Learning Experience, I guess I'll take it. I just have to remind myself that I could be teaching college English, or unloading trucks for a living (two jobs I've held that needed improvement), and accept what the universe offers.

Finding success as a writer takes hard work and commitment. Each person defines success differently, and each embarks on a different path. But even though we're traveling separately, we writers can help each other on the journey—which is what I hope *Dojo Wisdom for Writers* has done for you, helped you on your way.

Take to heart the lessons that spoke to you and discard the rest. Focus on the ideas, suggestions and sentiments that seem most helpful to you right now . . . and write now. Come back later if you've hit a roadblock or start to waver in your quest. I hope you'll find the encouragement you need to continue on.

And most of all . . . *Pilsung!*

Resources

For more information, visit Jennifer Lawler at www.jenniferlawler.com or call her toll-free number, 1-877-THE DOJO.

Trade Associations and Professional Groups

American Society of Journalists and Authors
1501 Broadway, Suite 302
New York, NY 10036
212-997-0947   www.asja.org

Authors Guild
330 West 42nd Street
New York, NY 10036
212-268-1208   www.authors-guild.org

Home Office Association of America
909 Third Avenue
New York, NY 10022
800-809-4622   www.hoaa.com

National Association of Home Based Businesses
10451 Mills Run Circle, #400
Owing Mills, MD 21117
410-363-3698   www.usahomebiz.com

National Association for the Self-Employed
2121 Precinct Line Road
Hurst, TX 76054
800-232-6273   www.nase.org

National Association of Women Writers
P.O. Box 183812
Arlington, TX 76096
866-821-5829   www.naww.org

National Writers Union
113 University Place, Sixth Floor
New York, NY 10003
212-254-0279   www.nwu.org

Society of Children's Book Writers and Illustrators
8271 Beverly Boulevard
Los Angeles, CA 90048
323-782-1010   www.scbwi.org

Writers Guild of America East
555 West 57th Street
New York, NY 10019
212-767-7800   www.wga.org

Writers Guild of America West
7000 West Third Street
Los Angeles, CA 90048
213-951-4000   www.wga.org

Helpful People and Organizations

Volunteer Lawyers for the Arts
www.starvingartistslaw.com

'Lectric Law Library
www.lectlaw.com

Find Law
www.findlaw.com

Publishers Weekly
Information on the trade
www.publishersweekly.com

Publishers Lunch
Daily e-newsletter about book deals
www.publisherslunch.com

Who Represents?
A website for finding which agents represent which writers
www.whorepresents.com

Publicity Advisor
www.publicityadvisor.com

PR Leads subscription service
www.prleads.com

For finding newspaper websites:
www.newspaperlinks.com

For finding media links:
www.kidon.com/medialink/index.htm

Recommended Reading

Bly, Robert. *Secrets of a Freelance Writer.* New York: Holt, 1997.

Bowerman, Peter. *The Well-Fed Writer.* Atlanta: Fanove Publishing, 2000.

Camenson, Blythe, and Marshall J. Cook. *Your Novel Proposal: From Creation to Contract.* Cincinnati, Ohio: Writer's Digest Books, 1999.

Cameron, Julia. *The Artist's Way: A Spiritual Path to Higher Creativity.* New York: Tarcher, 1992.

Children's Writer's and Illustrator's Market. Cincinnati, Ohio: Writer's Digest Books, annual.

Clausen, John. *Too Lazy to Work, Too Nervous to Steal: How to Have a Great Life as a Freelance Writer.* Cincinnati, Ohio: Writer's Digest Books, 2001.

Cook, Marshall. *Freeing Your Creativity.* Cincinnati, Ohio: Writer's Digest Books, 1995.

Editors of Story Press. *Idea Catcher.* Cincinnati, Ohio: Story Press, 1998.

Formichelli, Linda, and Diana Burrell. *The Renegade Writer.* Oak Park, Ill.: Marion Street Press, 2003.

Foster, Jack. *How to Get Ideas.* San Francisco: Berrett-Koehler Publishing, 1996.

Gerard, Philip. *Writing a Book That Makes a Difference.* Cincinnati, Ohio: Story Press, 2000.

Herman, Jeff. *Writer's Guide to Book Publishers, Editors, and Literary Agents.* New York: Prima, 2003.

James-Enger, Kelly. *Ready, Aim, Specialize.* New York: Writer, 2003.

King, Stephen. *On Writing.* New York: Pocket, 2002.

Kremer, John. *1001 Ways to Market Your Books.* Fairfield, Iowa: Open Horizons Publishing, 1998.

Lamott, Anne. *Bird by Bird: Some Instructions on Writing and Life.* New York: Anchor, 1995.

Leland, Christopher T. *The Art of Compelling Fiction.* Cincinnati, Ohio: Story Press, 1998.

Levinson, Jay Conrad, et al. *Guerrilla Marketing for Writers.* Cincinnati, Ohio: Writer's Digest Books, 2001.

Lukeman, Noah. *The First Five Pages.* New York: Fireside, 2000.

Maisel, Eric. *Fearless Creating.* New York: Putnam, 1995.

Photographer's Market. Cincinnati, Ohio: Writer's Digest Books, annual.

Rose, M. J., and Angela Adair-Hoy. *How to Publish and Promote Online.* New York: St. Martin's, 2001.

Ross, Marilyn, and Tom Ross. *Jump Start Your Book Sales.* Buena Vista, Colo.: Communications Creativity, 1999.

Songwriter's Market. Cincinnati, Ohio: Writer's Digest Books, annual.

Stein, Sol. *Stein on Writing.* New York: St. Martin's, 1995.

Warren, Lissa. *The Savvy Author's Guide to Book Publicity.* New York: Carroll and Graf, 2004.

Writer's Market. Cincinnati, Ohio: Writer's Digest Books, annual.